SHEEBA'S
SECRET

SHEEBA'S
SECRET

A Formula for More Success Through Greater Self-Awareness

SHEEBA VARGHESE

BPS books

Toronto and New York
www.bpsbooks.com

Published in 2011 by
BPS Books
Toronto and New York
www.bpsbooks.com
A division of Bastian Publishing Services Ltd.

ISBN 978-1-926645-65-0

Cataloguing-in-Publication Data available from Library
and Archives Canada.

Cover: Gnibel
Text design and typesetting: Daniel Crack, Kinetics Design, www.kdbooks.ca

Printed by Lightning Source, Tennessee. Lightning Source paper,
as used in this book, does not come from endangered old-growth forests
or forests of exceptional conservation value. It is acid free, lignin free, and
meets all ANSI standards for archival-quality paper. The print-on-demand
process used to produce this book protects the environment by printing
only the number of copies that are purchased.

This book is more than my secret; it is my life.

I dedicate it and all future successes to my babies,

Jared and Sage. May you both grow to be

the people you were designed to be.

Contents

Part 4 Success

Preface

OVER the past decade my life has been deeply touched by the many clients and others I've been associated with as a coach and friend. Each of you has confirmed that, regardless of who we are or where we find ourselves, we're all hardwired to want more, to progress, to be successful and fulfilled – all at the same time. My thanks to all of you who have allowed me to be part of your journey on the way to more in your life, and to Jared, Sage, and Stephen for your support.

Introduction

What This Book Can Do for You

F**OR** the better part of a year, I could be found at my Starbucks in Oakville enjoying a Grande Bold and working on this book. Writing is a solitary process; writing in a public space was therefore interesting. True, I have a natural tendency to engage with people, but answering the question "What are you working on?" sparked particularly rich discussions that reaffirmed my sense that people are looking for more success in their life – the subject of my book.

Through my company, Forward Focus Inc., I work as an executive coach with CEOs and senior executives across North America; we increase their success by increasing their self-awareness. This book shares my story and elements of their stories, including the challenges we've faced along the way. (Names of clients have been changed, as well as details of their situation, to protect their privacy.) While I work primarily with executives, the secret of success through self-awareness can work for everyone, whatever their position in life.

The biggest takeaway for me from a decade of coaching is the simple and powerful truth that *success comes through self-awareness*. Regardless of our job title – whether we're the president or looking for work – true success requires greater self-knowledge. We can have lots of external success – money, partners, friends, babies, trips, and toys – and still feel empty inside. We can read the right books and get inspired – and then be frustrated that nothing has changed. This book is for those who want more. It's for those who want the internal satisfaction that enables external success. Actually, it's for those who want it all – success in body, mind, and soul – and who are ready to take action to get it.

Typically, clients sign up for executive coaching because they believe it will enable them to have more success as defined by external variables. They believe what the management books tell them – that it is concrete actions that will lead to tangible returns. I'm seeing a new trend, however, in which clients are using their *personal* profile and strengths to develop their action plans for more success at work. They see that the better they understand their "soft stuff" – personal desires, values, and objectives – the better all of their results will be, including the "hard stuff."

Here are three important points about my approach and my work.

First, I focus on the being, not the doing, side of life.

Many executive coaches have been given the mandate to focus on doing, through strategy and execution. Let's say, for example, an organization engages them to work with its executives to increase their effectiveness in their roles. The coaches may concentrate on sharpening the executives' communication and time-management skills based on their tasks, responsibilities, and objectives. Most of these coaches have been in the very role of the executives they're coaching, often in the same industry. This type of development usually fails to motivate or inspire people to look at their life from a less obvious perspective and limits the return such an investment could have.

In contrast, my clients come to me not through human resources departments but through my own networking and by word of mouth. The mandate for my work, therefore, arises from where the clients are in their lives. Many of my clients are decades older than I am. They don't come to me expecting me to share industry knowledge or years of experience as a CEO, even though I do possess these things. I take my nine-month contract with them very seriously and know this may be the first time they've ever looked, holistically, at their effectiveness and success. To that point, it's not uncommon for many of my clients to continue with me past the first nine-month contract.

Greater success for you lies in your willingness to grow as a person, to develop a deeper understanding of who you are. This is of utmost importance because everything else flows and extends from who you are.

Second, I invite you to engage more with your life.

It's okay for you to want more in your life. Most people think they're the only ones struggling to realize the success they want in the totality of their lives. In fact, many feel they're not even *allowed* to want more. Nothing is broken and so they feel they should feel happy enough.

We already know life can trip any of us up, and when we remember that, we're better able to deal with our setbacks and engage more with our lives.

I wish I had known all of this much earlier in my life, because I felt very alone. If it weren't for the modicum of self-knowledge I already had, I probably wouldn't have changed my life in meaningful ways. Most of the people I turned to in my search for more feared for me, doubted me, and told me I was a fool. But they didn't really know me; I had to remind myself I was the only one who knew how I felt and wanted to feel.

Setbacks are less frightening when we're better equipped in body, mind, and soul. You have all it takes to realize your visions and aspirations or you wouldn't have them. The more knowledge you have of who you are, the better equipped you will be to deal with your setbacks, visions, and aspirations. An equal amount of gain is available to you from within the chaos your journey may cause, if you use your creativity and curiosity to find it and then use your knowledge of self to leverage it.

So dare to want more and be prepared for some tough and fulfilling work to get it. Take action. You're the only one who can create the kind of change you desire. To be really clear on your opportunities for more, you'll need to be clear on the opportunities for your life right now. Unless you look in the mirror with a willingness to see the good, the bad, and the ugly, how long might that lettuce stay stuck between your teeth? Work on what you don't necessarily adore in what you see peering back at you.

And third, the insights I share are the result of my own experience – much of it confusing and difficult – in achieving success. I didn't want success for me to include hurting others, and yet I had to find the courage to make some tough decisions to live in sync with my deepest values. Otherwise my life would have been the same old, same old: a variation of a standard life based on external models and expectations. I have written this book to invite you to have the courage to make things different in your life.

I'm sharing this book with you because as a citizen of this world – as an active member of society, part of a visible minority, a single mom, a successful entrepreneur, and an executive coach – I've learned the secret of the direct connection between our personal understanding of who we are and the quality of our existence. Bottom line: Self-awareness enables success.

Here's the formula we'll be exploring together in this book:

$$\textit{Self-Awareness + Focus + Strategy}$$
$$\textit{= \textbf{SUCCESS}}$$

I take you through the self-awareness, focus, and strategy elements of the formula in the first three parts of this book, and the success element in the fourth part. I devote some time in the early chapters to my own story because we learn from each other's journeys.

So gather your strength, and brace yourself. Know in advance that the journey to self-discovery for personal growth and success is stimulating, exciting, interesting, and lonely – all at the same time. It's also the richest journey you'll ever take.

Part 1

Self-Awareness

$$\begin{array}{r} \textbf{\textit{Self-Awareness}} \\ + \qquad \textit{Focus} \\ + \qquad \textit{Strategy} \\ \hline \textbf{\textit{= SUCCESS}} \end{array}$$

Chapter 1
A Journey Begins

*All I can do is act according to
my deepest instinct, and be
whatever I must be – crazy or
ribald or sad or compassionate
or loving or indifferent.
That is all anybody can do.*

–Katharine Butler Hathaway

IN business, the "soft stuff" – for example, the values of inclusiveness, fairness, kindness, meaning, and growth of self – has typically been overlooked in favor of hardcore stuff – increasing shareholder value and focusing strategically on what contributes to a higher return on investment (ROI). The soft stuff, which can also include values like integrity, stimulation, excitement, and discovery, is usually denied to business leaders because it seems to lie outside the world of tangible, measurable results. There are lots of reasons for this. Dismissing the soft stuff in favor of ROI is completely misguided, however. Think about it. CEOs and senior executives are traditionally the strongest people in our society in terms of assertiveness, boldness, vision, communication, and laser-focused responsiveness. These people are the straws that stir our drinks. They're our employers, running the companies whose taxes fund our societies. The collective is screwed when these leaders deny the critical importance of their personal development.

Soft Stuff, Hard Stuff

My approach leads with the acknowledgment that every aspect of our life factors into our business, career, and life success. That should be obvious because, regardless of how much we may wish or try to forget it, we're more than the roles we perform. Those who prefer to think that's all they are limit themselves in every area of their life – including their role. Sometimes my clients want to focus on their corporate objectives only. But real, meaningful, and sustainable development, growth, and results require factoring in the bigger life picture. Most of my clients realize gains far beyond the context of their work because they're finally focusing on who they are as a person.

Studies show only fifteen percent of people in the world possess the leadership abilities that drive change. Of that group, maybe three percent want to get to the next level in their *personal* evolution of self and excellence to be better leaders. It baffles me why it plays out this way. Perhaps it's because it requires exploring the soft stuff, a process that's unfamiliar and therefore uncomfortable, or perhaps because they don't understand how the soft skills are integrally related to the hard skills. Generally speaking, we have relegated the soft stuff focus to women. Big strong men go out and work to bring home the day's provisions. We seem to have forgotten that both men and women evolve and want more than what they've traditionally known. We as women have found our voice and no longer allow men to try dragging us back into the caves by our hair. Now men must decide how *they* will evolve.

There's a powerful business case for this focus. The five key components of high performance are education, experience, skills, personality, and intelligence. Most high performers are not that far apart on any of these five components except the wild-card variable of personality. Yet personality – which is where the soft skills reside – is the biggest influencer of results that go beyond good to great. The business case is that focusing on soft skills increases personal fulfillment, which gets people over the top to better and more sustainable results in their roles.

This truth has been confirmed for me in my professional life. I became the CEO of Forward Focus Professional Coaching Services at thirty-one years of age. Under my leadership, Forward Focus has emerged as one of the most respected coaching organizations in Canada. Using my sales background, I have worked hard to make my company a strong, lucrative, results-oriented organization. This during a time when the market had little understanding of the coaching profession or of me and my unique approach to the profession.

Since then I've been profiled by national and regional media, including on the cover of a business magazine for my involvement on the Prime Minister of Canada's Task Force on Women Entrepreneurs. In 2009 I was nominated for the Caldwell/*Globe and Mail* Top 40 Under 40 in Canada, for my business success. Under my leadership, Forward Focus Inc. has expanded to include a larger platform through an Internet-based TV show, *More Focus Inc.* (www.morefocus.tv), and now this book. I'm an invited speaker on the topic of success and self-awareness.

Three Defining Moments

We are all a function of our experiences and there is value in understanding them. The personal journey that got me here involves three defining moments that have shaped much of my perspective.

First, a little background.

My dad is a United Church minister and comes from Kerala, India. (Yes, it's possible to be a Christian and from India.) We always lived in small white communities. This was never really a problem for me, even though small-town Canadian life during the years from 1970 to the beginning of the 1990s made us a *very* visible minority. The white families around us knew there were African Canadians out there somewhere, but brown people? We weren't studied in school. We were the Great Unknown.

Girls, however, always seemed to like my tall, dark, handsome brothers, who seemed to be more successful than I in negotiating the great cultural divide. Or maybe it felt more difficult to me because I was the only girl in a family with four brothers. We never discussed our situation as siblings or as a family; it's likely everyone had their own issues to deal with.

I was generally popular at school, yet guys were never interested in me romantically. That was embarrassing and tough for me, because they were always my friends. Particularly in my teen years, the years that most build a person's character and identity, I felt I didn't have much to build on. My sense of equilibrium was off. I focused on being like the other girls. This objective was completely unattainable for a brown girl in a sea of white.

Not only that, I seemed to have been cursed with an overabundance of facial hair for a girl. This caused me much despair. There I was, clearly different from everyone else because I was brown and had a mustache. And my name was one people seemed to like giving to their dogs. What sibling could resist such a great opportunity for teasing? Oh yes, add chicken legs to the mix and you have a pretty good idea of the subterranean level of my self-esteem. The only measurements I knew to apply to myself were shallow physical ones.

Defining Moment #1

I think I was fifteen when my brother Jamie told me I needed to be prepared for my life.

"You're so ugly, you'd better develop a personality or else you're going to be screwed," he said.

His words were invaluable to me. They gave me a different perspective. He and my other brothers were always telling me I was ugly. Rarely was it ever suggested otherwise, so I knew I needed to heed what Jamie had told me. His words gave me hope. They suggested that maybe the physical was just one piece of a person's identity. Now I had a sense of how I could focus my efforts. Far from devastating me, his words eased my feelings of helplessness.

So I set about to do what he said – until I realized I didn't know how to develop a personality.

I thought my best bet was to be known as the sister of my cute, cool, athletic brothers and as a person of energy, sociability, and boldness. That seemed to work. Soon I was accepted with only a personality. My longing, however, was to be liked for being a girl like all my beautiful friends. I just kept hoping for a better day and developed ways to leverage my assets and minimize my defects. I kept my hand over my mouth when I was close to others and changed my name from Sheeba to keep people from associating me with their pets.

Defining Moment #2

My dad liked to change his parishes every seven years or so. My last move with the family, in 1988, at the end of my grade eleven year, was tough for me. I was leaving a school where I was popular and involved in sports and the student council. In the previous moves, all of us kids had been affected. This time it was really just me. My older brothers had either finished university or were still in it, and my younger brother, Joshua, was just starting grade one. Grade twelve turned out to be better than I thought but I was still looking for something more.

I had become acquainted in my earlier high school years with some exchange students and was intrigued by the idea of going abroad and learning a new language. John, my eldest brother, had spent a year in Birmingham, England, on a work exchange with his university. Establishing myself somewhere far away seemed like a great adventure.

I put the wheels in motion, and off I went, before the beginning of the 1989-90 school year, to Liège, Belgium, as a Rotary Exchange student.

This experience changed my life. I learned French, saw Europe, and for the first time in any significant way was appreciated by men. In Europe, they loved East Indian women, facial hair and all! In the safety of my three great host families and the Amay-Villers-le-Temple Rotary Club, I caught a glimpse of the kind of journey my life could take.

At Thanksgiving of that year, John, who had been instrumental in getting me to Europe, called and suggested I come home early to finish my last semester of high school; if I didn't do that, I'd end up having to take a whole year of high school before university, he reminded me.

"The time you have spent in Europe will always be a good memory for you," he said. "But think about what you'll be coming back to. Think about how hard it will be for you to come home and spend a whole year back at home with Dad."

John understood that our father's only reference point was India and his three older *sons*. He laid out the reality I needed to be prepared for. He also said it was my choice and my choice alone.

"If you do stay," he said, "I don't want to hear you complaining about how tough it is when you get back, since I warned you."

Making this tough decision at eighteen years of age was my second defining moment. I had to consider the consequences I was willing to accept against what I was gaining and wanted to experience. As in the case of my first defining moment, I had to consider my life more strategically.

I remember thinking John was more detail-oriented than I was. I wondered if my big-picture perspective was the right one for making this decision. I tried taking his approach and focused on the more visible short term. I almost went home. But then I decided to do my own assessment of the risks. I considered the costs and benefits of staying. In the end I decided to stick with *my* perspective and finish my year abroad.

My decision set off a series of events and consequences that inform everything I do to this very day. I made the right decision for me because I used the only filter that mattered: *my own.*

I also made a very important discovery as a result of staying. I wanted a good life like that of my host families. I began to see the relationship between their lives and what they did for a living. I traced what they did for a living to the fact they had done better than average in high school so they could get into the right school to study their chosen profession. Now I was getting why it was important to care about school. I needed to pull up my socks so I could get into a good university and have a great life.

Back home at the beginning of the 1990-91 school year, I was introduced to a new and unexpected kind of freedom, one that was different from what I had known even as an exchange student. Yes, this new freedom was cosmetic and superficial – and had a huge impact on my confidence.

My friend Tanya's dad owned a beauty salon, and one day she waxed my mustache off. I didn't even know this was possible. I thought I had been born with a lifelong curse. Now I felt I had a new chance at life. No more covering my mouth when close to others. I displayed my hairless upper lip with pride – to teachers, friends, parents, kids, even strangers on the street. Who would have thought such a simple procedure could have such an effect on me?

This may not seem like much to you if you've always been cute or attractive, but for me it was release from a life sentence. I was finally free to imagine being a normal girl. According to Maslow's Hierarchy of Needs, when our lower-level needs for this kind of social belonging and acceptance are met, we can move on to the bigger, more meaningful pursuits in life. I now felt fully acceptable socially. The future was limitless: Bilingual in French and English, ready to get serious about school, and no mustache – I was unstoppable!

The ideals my first two defining moments instilled in me continue to serve me well. I still care more about my character and the character of others than about physical looks. The decision to stay in Europe showed me I was able to comfortably take risks and that my thought processes were sound. I understood what it meant to be a calculated risk-taker: It was natural for me to weigh the potential conse-quences of a worst-case scenario, and to consider the costs and the benefits of different options. These learnings have been instrumental in shaping my life and my character.

Defining Moment #3

In February 1991, six months after my return from Belgium, I was in a serious motor vehicle accident, and the future suddenly became "less limitless." I was driving my dad's car when a tire blew and the car lost control, crashing through a fence and hitting a tree. The rescue team had to use the Jaws of Life to get me out. I was in and out of a coma for two weeks and lived in various hospitals for the next three months.

The crash left me with severe head injuries – the frontal lobe of my brain was seriously damaged – along with severe bone collapse to the left side of my face, double vision (which I still have today because of the trauma to the brain), a broken foot, and some other less serious injuries. And yet this was truly one of the best things that ever happened to me. I lost the part of the brain that governs reward, attention, short-term memory tasks, planning, and drive-related abilities. This handicap has been negligible for me. I seem to have been blessed with insights and abilities that more than compensate for what I lost.

Sailing into Sales

After graduating from university in 1995 I didn't have any better idea of what I wanted my life to be about. My degree – a mix of French, psychology, and a smattering of business – reflected my lack of clarity. In Belgium I had told the Rotarians I was going to be the Prime Minister of Canada and a journalist. All I really ever knew to know was that I needed to earn lots of money so I could live a good life and that I made decisions best in my own space. In my twentieth year, I reclaimed my name, Sheeba.

I made it through university with the confidence of my new self, the special needs office, note-takers, and an amazing boyfriend, who became my husband and the father of my two children. Jeff had graduated a year before me and was already working in a great job for him, in London, Ontario. Jeff and I, who were friends from high school and dated in university, had become engaged during my last year of university.

As I considered the possibilities that most appealed to me, my romantic ideal was to return to Europe. Jeff knew our town in Ontario was not my first choice geographically. He encouraged me to find ways to make our place and lives feel like Europe.

I went into sales because selling was easy for me and I knew it could lead me to almost any job.

And just like that, my life became like the lives around me. My dad helped Jeff and me to buy a house immediately after we got married. The two of us had good jobs, were paying down our mortgage, attended a nice church, and had a lovely garden. I even buzzed around in a cute little sports car.

In my first sales role out of university, Paul, a client who is still a friend, helped me expand my reference points to include the teachings of such people as Brian Tracy, Jack Boland, Earl Nightingale, and James Allen, which led me to A Course in Miracles and then to the objectivist philosophy of Ayn Rand. I couldn't get enough of this unknown world of true potential, possibility, and truth. I engaged with it anywhere and everywhere, even with my sales clients, who ate it up, too.

For the first five years after university I averaged one job a year. I quit some of these jobs with Jeff's blessing and was let go from a few others for various reasons. With no role models to relate to, I approached jobs like an amateur betting on horses, picking at random and hoping for the best. I tried working for big multinationals. I tried selling more challenging products. Nothing I did seemed the right fit for me.

Around this time, at my brother John's suggestion, I read *What Color Is Your Parachute?* This famous career book did nothing to lift the fog of my confusion, so clearly the problem was me. The only thing I knew was I wanted to feel more satisfaction with my life. That meant more sales jobs, because they seemed to fit my style and could be as vague as my degree. (But at least I did have my degree.)

Enter: Coaching

During this time, my brother Philip asked me if I had ever heard of the profession called coaching. He showed me an article about it in the *Globe and Mail*. Philip felt coaching would be compatible with my style. I decided to learn more. When I couldn't find a coach myself who could challenge me as a serious, results-oriented person with high drive, a sense of urgency, and little sense of direction, I decided to learn more about this profession and then looked into becoming one myself. I eventually found a coach and enrolled in night and weekend courses in coaching. I trained with two different institutions.

And so by 2001, all was well. I had given birth to my wonderful boy, Jared, and was on a year of maternity leave, which gave me time to finish my professional certification as a coach and begin working more actively with clients.

While still on maternity leave, I became pregnant with my wonderful second child, Sagesse. It was expected I would take another year of maternity leave, but my first leave had confirmed for me that I was not the stay-at-home type. Five months into this pregnancy, and with Jeff's blessing, I decided to start my own coaching business. I promised him if I didn't find enough clients within thirty days I would return to my well-paying job in order to have another paid maternity leave.

So I used my sales skills and went bowling for opportunities and dollars. I ended up securing a great client: an international retailer and its leadership team. Working as a coach with this client was exciting, meaningful, and lucrative. Clearly this was where I was supposed to be. I started my company, Forward Focus, in 2002, and chose as my tagline *Because There's More*, in response to the frequently asked question, "Why would I work with a coach?"

Chapter 2
Reality Check

*Few are they who have
never had the chance
to achieve happiness ...
and fewer those who have
taken that chance.*

–André Maurois

AND then a reality check – one that contributed greatly to my emerging understanding of the importance of self-awareness.

I worked with the leadership team and its team members for the remaining four months of my pregnancy. After giving birth to Sage, I took a few months to be a full-time mom, then hired a nanny and jumped back into the cold calling chair. This time, though, nothing seemed to work. No one was interested

in my services. I was confused. I had achieved almost immediate success the first time, and now, nothing.

My lack of success and the attitude of most people that
they didn't need a coach caused me to question my entrepreneurial decision and new career. At the same time, coaching
felt so meaningful, so results-focused, and pure. I knew this
was the type of work I wanted in my life. Coaching met my
needs and gave me the opportunity to work with those who
wanted more in their lives.

A Flawed Strategy

Business development was challenging so I accepted just
about any client who came my way or I could find. This was
not a good strategy. Many of these clients were blowhards:
people who claimed to want to be their best as long as it
didn't require too much heavy lifting. My corporate clients
paid big bucks and expected me to make their short people
tall and their tall people short. Sometimes it worked – and in
one particular case, it didn't. The company knew this person
wasn't a keeper. They were giving him one last chance to
prove them wrong. Using my sales skills, I sold them on
the benefits of coaching. And then I failed to deliver on my
promise.

This experience forced me to look at my model from a
more critical perspective. I couldn't afford to hurt my reputation and credibility. I needed to regroup and refocus and
remind myself why I was doing what I was doing. I remem-
bered the words of a former vice president of sales with whom
I worked in Calgary, Jean Kipp, who said, "When we're good
at what we do, the money follows." Sure enough, things
began to look up a little when I decided to focus my time
and efforts on finding clients who had depth to their being,
valued results, and wanted progress, straight talk, and honest
feedback – people who were ready for more in their lives.

This proved to be strategic because the majority of those who are hardwired this way are leaders – the ones who wield the most power and influence in their organizations. I focused on this niche and became an executive coach. I was surprised at the direction my life was taking but knew it was a great fit for me. I am intense, have a strong sense of urgency, and am driven to look at things from a big-picture perspective and achieve results. Business acumen and out-of-the-box insights complete a package that can be a tangible value-add for the right CEOs and senior executives – those who can get past the potential age and gender gap, that is.

While it was a better fit for me, this "ah-ha" moment did not translate into immediate results, whether in the quality of my clients or the velocity of my cash flow. I got it, though: My conviction was being tested. Even though I hated not being super-busy and making tons of money, I kept my focus on *finding the clients I needed in order to feel engaged and successful*. I plastered the walls of my office with my new approach and slogan: *Trust vs. Control*.

The Big Decision

We are whole people. When something is out of whack in one area, it naturally affects other areas of our lives. In case you disagree, ask someone who knows you how you show up when you're well-rested compared with when you're not. I had always controlled as much as I could in my life; I believed this was the only way to get what I wanted. Control didn't net me much joy or self-satisfaction, though, or at least not enough.

Once again the questions resurfaced about my life and what I wanted out of it. I knew I was married to a wonderful man. I lacked nothing. He treated me like gold. He was a wonderful father and always supported me in anything I wanted to do. He enabled me to develop a sense of myself so I could realize more of who I wanted to be. I was finally valued for being *me*. God, my kids, my marriage to Jeff, and my dog were the only things I was sure of and valued.

Hence my confusion when I was revisited by the visions I had tried to ignore throughout the ten years of our marriage and two years of dating. The visions reflected me as living a solitary life, which had been my reality for the first twenty or so years of my life. I had always seen myself as a gypsy, a free spirit traveling through life, exploring, discovering, growing in specific ways, adventurous, and bold. I was inspired and motivated by a set of values different from the ones underpinning my current life. I was married "till death do us part," yet the values that defined my personality would not have me commit to anything, other than my babies, till death.

I knew it was in everyone's best interest for me to make peace with where I was. I knew no one wins when there's a lack of integrity in our actions. I knew Jeff deserved more. I wanted to be inspired by my own life. I wanted to live in personal integrity. It was useless for me to blame myself. It wasn't as if I wanted to make my life tougher. And so, rather than spend my time and energy trying to force myself to be someone I was not destined to be, I finally surrendered to who I really was.

Our kids were quite little, ages four and five, when I began having focused discussions with Jeff about our alignment and compatibility. Man I struggled. By this time I was in my mid-thirties. Some people already considered me to be too much and this just proved their case. I received little support from family and friends. That's not surprising. They may have rushed to my side if I was leaving a man who was a boozer, womanizer, abuser, or jerk. All they could see was a self-employed mother with young children and a young company leaving a man who was innocent.

The more solid information we have about who we are, the better we can live a life on our own terms. My flawed approach to life represented the convergence of my lack of understanding of life, my low self-esteem, and my ignorance of my values and real identity. I had never thought my wants and needs were important enough to consider, for the big things. I planned my life logically because that seemed the safe way to achieve the good, stable life that society tells us to strive for. When it came to big decisions, I wanted to hear what others thought and desired before I expressed my take on the situation. That's a wise strategy, especially when done with confidence, not self-doubt. I had been raised by strong, sharp-tongued men and feared stepping out of line. External models and expectations had dictated how my life was lived. Since everyone seemed to have better reference points than I did, I tried to follow where the external models and expectations led.

Now, during my training as a coach and early years in the profession, I was growing in my knowledge of self. I was learning the importance of values. At first I thought they were just words; words people thought were noble or good. Discovering my values was both the best and worst thing I could have done. I started to understand what was causing my nagging thoughts: my lack of commitment to my own values.

Further, I was beginning to see the misalignment between my values and Jeff's. Alignment is when our essence, our *being*, shows up naturally in everything we're *doing*. Without a solid sense of our being, of who we are, our choices are hit-and-miss. Society wants us to tolerate these odds for the sake of the collective. Many of us choose to go through the motions in our work life. And as couples we ignore the elephant we have invited into the room by relegating our discussions and decisions to the kids, home improvements, and vacations.

I didn't want to have to make the choices I did, and at the same time it wasn't just about me anymore. It was also about what I wanted my children to grow up knowing. I wanted them to know we're in choice each day of our lives; that we choose to live, or to go through the motions. I believe God is compassionate. He recognizes we made many of our key choices without really knowing what we were choosing, without knowing who we really were, without understanding that to fully enjoy everything life has to offer us, we must honor our full design.

Once I got really clear about my desire to live the remainder of my life on my terms and by my values, I took definitive action and ended our marriage.

And Now?

Jeff is happily remarried to Jen, a woman I believe to be a better wife for him. They're more aligned in their values and dreams. Our children have responded well, though it's not always easy for them. I have a very close relationship with both of them and get along well with Jeff and Jen. I learned in my research that children adjust better to divorces when they're younger because they do not yet have as strong a reference point of Mom and Dad together. My kids and I do so much together, including sleeping, playing, and talking, and I'm active and involved in their activities and school. I've even coached Jared's flag football team and Sage's soccer team with Jen.

Sage, who is now seven, suggested I include a chapter in this book on divorce, to "let people who are afraid know it all works out and it does not have to be bad." There's more value in Sage writing that book from a kid's perspective. She works on it when I'm available to be her scribe. Watch for it. *Tuesdays Thursdays and Every Other Weekend* is the title, reflecting the kids' schedule with their dad. These kids are amazing and an intricate part of me. They accept me with my values and choices. I want them to learn that conviction for something always comes at a cost, and they get to choose. I've chosen to teach them integrity over tradition.

Five years have passed and my business has benefited from my personal journey, and vice versa. Great things keep happening as I stay true to my values. My platform has added an Internet show, www.morefocus.tv, and an exciting pilot of another show, along with this book, at the request of the Fox and NBC TV networks in the U.S. Regardless of how all this plays out, it shows me the limitlessness of life when we lead with our values, whatever they may be.

A Path of Self-Discovery

I travel often from my base in Toronto, Canada, to meet clients. For over two years I flew biweekly to Calgary to work with the executives of an oil and gas company. On one of my trips there my seat mate was someone I recognized from TV and had seen in concert and heard often on the radio: Jim Cuddy, the lead singer of Blue Rodeo. He was heading out to perform at the Juno Awards.

Jim and I talked about people in a general way and about the coaching process. Later, he was a guest on my show, during which we focused on the value of freedom as we spoke about how his values have played out in his life. (You can view his interview online at www.morefocus.tv.)

He told me in an e-mail he sent me after the show about a new song on the band's *Things We Left Behind* CD. It was called "Sheba," he said. It was primarily influenced by the Queen of Sheba and "maybe just a little by the lovely, forceful woman I met on a plane."

I was so excited to think I had played even a small part in inspiring a song. I got the CD and was blown away that the whole song was about our plane ride. Here's how the chorus goes:

I know
I think about it all the time though
There's nothing really for me to hold on to
I'm taking the days as they come
I'm right here
Stuck between a dream and a nightmare
Praying for the day when it all comes clear
I'm barely just holding my ground
Til Sheba comes down

What struck me most was how the song captures the journey of my clients – in fact, of every one of us. We're all on a path of self-discovery. Some of us have it forced on us by health or marital breakdowns; others choose to focus on one day at a time rather than consider the more that's possible in life; and others – among whose ranks I hope you number – actively *seek* it.

WHAT ABOUT YOU?

- *Which of your thoughts do you understand least?*

- *How do these thoughts leave you feeling?*

- *How often do you look at the whole of your life?*

- *How much of your life satisfies you?*

- *Do you know what could satisfy you more?*

- *What's preventing you from exploring these possibilities?*

Chapter 3

Good or Great?

*Where the willingness is great,
the difficulties cannot be great.*

–Niccolo Machiavelli

IF you're among those who are satis-fied with the good you have in your life and that's all you sincerely want, then be where you are and put this book away.

If you want to live a more joyful, fulfilling, and successful life, then be prepared to travel farther down the winding path of greater self-awareness.

Good vs. Great

Most people choose good because it's good. That's the unspoken standard we've all agreed to value to ensure the stability of society. People in the collective want to maintain the status quo. They have no interest in adding ambiguity, change, or risk to their current realities. They feel – and want to continue feeling – comfortable, safe, and secure.

It's when people decide to go beyond good to great, however, that their true paths begin to reveal themselves.

If you're truly in pursuit of greatness, be vigilant. Don't compromise your standards or limit your potential by being satisfied with good, unless that's the maximum of what's available. Straddling both sides of good and great can be an effective enough strategy – until it stops satisfying you and you can't stand any longer how it makes you feel. It's when we commit ourselves to greatness that our lives take on new meaning. How satisfied are you with your life? Is your life good or great? What's missing? What feelings do you want to have more frequently?

Consider taking an inside-out approach, from your *being* to your *doing*. This approach to life requires a deeper focus on self-understanding. Even just a basic level of self-understanding can be useful, revealing what helps and what hinders us. A deeper level of self-understanding, however, enables us to clarify our values, which are our ticket to sustainable success.

How important is it to you to feel happier about yourself and your life? Does getting to know yourself more deeply feel too risky? The other option, as you already know, is to keep going along to get along – to keep putting other people's needs/feelings and values ahead of your own. Your elders, parents, church, or schools may have taught you this reference point. Ask yourself, though, how well it worked for them. If it didn't, ask yourself why they would encourage you to follow their same flawed mental models. The fact is, in a classic case of the blind leading the blind, they don't necessarily know why they did what they did. It's even worse when those who *can* see still choose to follow the blind.

It's no one's fault we make such big life decisions with

such little actual awareness/information of who we are. It's our responsibility to address the situation, though.

Of course, risk is always associated with any change we make. Will it work out?

What if it *did* work out for you? What would you stand to gain?

We limit ourselves anytime we make choices based only on what's in front of us. When we hold on to those choices, after acknowledging we want more, we lose our zest for life and let go of the opportunity for greatness.

What are you afraid of? What aspects of the status quo are you choosing? Do you really believe the status quo works? Is it working for you?

We live very long lives now. Whether you have another fifty years to go or ten, why not make those years the maximum you want them to be? Stop going through the motions of living a good life, knowing you should be happy and not really knowing what to do to feel that way.

There are consequences to any choice. When we sell out on ourselves, we're usually forced to deal with ones that could have been avoided with a little effort. Examine the dogmas you're living by. Don't just casually lean back and say *could have, should have, would have.* You can play your situation down all you want, but it won't change the reality of your situation, whatever it is. You get one kick at the can. Why not be all you are?

Perhaps living like your mother – taken care of by a man while you raise the children – was a legitimate or romantic choice. But what about your life post-kids? What will you do then?

Maybe marrying the hottie or cutie felt like a medal of honor and now you're finally willing to admit this person doesn't stimulate you to grow as a person or in any other way. What will you do?

Maybe the reason you spent all those hours on the golf

course or focusing on the kids was to help you deal with the rest of your life. You wouldn't take such a lazy, sloppy shot at success if this was your career or business we were talking about. You would plan better and learn more. You would avoid falling into pitfalls. Why not take this approach in your personal life, too? In fact, why not drive for maximum success in the whole of your life? The return on your investment will be so much greater.

What's the cost to you of not being in a reality that inspires you? How often are you surrounded by company you truly enjoy? How often do you have interesting, stimulating discussions that inspire you to grow as a person? How much do people enjoy *your* company? Are you enjoyed for what you *do* for others or for who you *are*?

If you haven't yet chosen the level of active, ongoing participation you want in the whole of your own life, chances are your life will be very controllable, predictable, and boring. Why? Because your choices will always follow the same flawed, prescribed models. Hey, if your choices are working for you and you sincerely believe and live by them, keep going. If they're no longer serving you, consider taking a more meaningful and productive journey.

And in case you think it's possible to compartmentalize your life and just focus on one area to minimize the others, may I remind you of that nursery song in which the knee bone's connected to the thigh bone and the thigh bone's connected to the hip bone ... Be clear: If you're out of sorts in one area of your life, it will affect your effectiveness in another area. That's just the way it works.

Good News

I ask prospective clients, as we're establishing whether they're a fit with my firm, to tell me a bit about their personal development efforts. People consider this a safe, standard line of questioning. Here's what I often hear:

"Oh yeah, when it comes to personal development and balance and all that stuff, I get to the gym every morning and take time in the morning to have my coffee and paper alone and use that time to focus. My wife gets the kids ready for school and deals with all that stuff before she goes to work, so I'm lucky that way because everyone's happy at home. I'm into a good groove; just got our stock evaluations and that picture looks good – we had a great third quarter – and so I'm taking a golf trip with the boys next week. So as long as everything is working at home, I keep my focus on work and client dinners."

Which being translated is: "I'm self-absorbed, not aware of anything much other than me. And I just want you to help me make more money so I continue looking good."

It's easier to be like these people and follow a prescribed external model of success. If optics are what you're most conscious of, your identity will be a function of what society deems as looking most respectable. You'll live for others and follow the same mental models.

Consider the personal cost you pay when you live this way. Why take such a lazy approach to your life? Take the time to stand for something. Have the courage to live in integrity to what you stand for.

The good news is, there seems to be an increase these days in the number of people who have had enough of their safe, prescribed travels. They're no longer willing to tolerate their dissatisfaction. They're seeking more personal fulfillment and peace. These people are finally turning inward. They're becoming more aware of their need for a new vision that will move them forward in their body, mind, and soul quest – a quest we're all on, whether we realize it yet or not. Spiritual, inside-out knowledge makes life easier and better. And it's fun, bold, and exciting.

If you subscribe to a Higher Power, as I do via God, know that there's little emphasis in that perspective on the specifics of your choices. It's up to you to make the choices you want to make. Just make them as wisely as you can to begin with. Get to know yourself before you get too far down those winding, bumpy paths of your life. Equip yourself for your journey from the inside out, not just with formal education or training, which is an outside-in approach.

He gave us free will. If he wanted everyone to be the same and make the same choices, then we'd all have the same personalities, values, and temperaments, as well as the same desires, goals, and strategies. He could have designed us that way, and he didn't. I think what matters most to God is that we be the people he designed us to be. He wants to see how we use our abilities. Some choose to just follow how they're led; others, thankfully, engage with their lives to discover who they are.

If he has specific objectives, places, and people he wants us to know and experience, surely as God, who can do anything, he will ensure these things happen. Trust that there's a plan, however loosely defined it may be. Know that you're not alone and that your job is to focus on making *you* happen.

You may already intuitively know what this book is stating and feel ready to go down this path to educate yourself more about yourself. That's the only way to win on your terms, the only way to have a successful life and feel peace inside. Do some due diligence now regardless of the stage of life you're in. Focus on who you are. New songs by Pink and Lady Gaga were released as I was completing this book. The message of their songs – the value of you, of how special you are, of your unique design – can be turned into mantras to help you love yourself. Sing them over and over. And know this: As you grow in your self-awareness – the knowledge of what makes you uniquely special at every level – you'll become even more powerful.

Having It All

As I was writing this book, I stopped working actively with new clients. Instead, I began conversing about soft stuff with anyone who approached me at the coffee shop. I was surprised by the number of people who acknowledged and accepted that they were just existing. The script they were following supported the status quo, dogma, tradition, fear, self-doubt, uncertainty, and desperation. They were just reacting to what life was throwing at them. I met so many women and men whose lives consist of taking directives from others. Is it any wonder fulfillment is so elusive to most?

Maybe you wonder what good it is to know there are possibilities in your life if you have little clue how to seize them. There's no disgrace in thinking you're directionless, because chances are you're not. Achieving a grasp, however slender, of what's great about you will help you find direction.

We all lose when we stifle other people's desires.

Even though we may not see it, we win when we encourage others to push for what they truly desire.

My attitude as a doer is like Phil Knight's of Nike: There comes a time when we must *just do it*. Woody Allen seconds this when he says we must push aside how we may be feeling and just get to work changing what we don't like. Allen also says eighty percent of success is showing up. That's all it takes to be on the path to having it all: making sure you show up in your own life, values and all. Those who do can never be considered directionless.

Having it all requires you to think longer, harder, and go deeper than you naturally do. It requires you to concentrate your focus and live intentionally. You'll feel great for taking a chance on yourself and getting started on this path. The universe is friendly to all of our objectives.

Getting to Know *You*

You have lived your life and realized a level of success. Congratulations for your achievements. By choosing this book, or being chosen for this book, you may well be open to considering how your approach could evolve to incorporate more *you*.

To do this you're going to have to challenge more of the processes you subscribe to. You're going to have to determine whether your approach is helping you find answers or perpetuating the problem. The more you consider the kind of experiences you want to realize, the better choices you will make. Why not affirm for yourself that you're setting yourself up for greatness by getting clearer on who you are from a traits perspective and developing your strategies based on this information? Don't accept regrets or keep saying, "If I knew then what I know now ..."

Get to know yourself. You'll be happier and live in truth.

I'm struck by how few of the people I meet and work with remain in the profession they prepared for in school. Many of them went down those paths in the first place under the influence of a parent or relative. Not much thought was given to their compatibility with that profession. How can such big decisions be made by someone other than the person who has to live and breathe the experience directly?

My clients are no slugs. They're top performers. They have achieved what society values. Yet few of them are satisfied personally. Who likes feeling that way? Who benefits?

Take a Chance on You

We live alone, we die alone, and we must make our own choices so we can accept the consequences with conviction. We can be guided, influenced, and challenged by others, *and* ultimately we must acknowledge and own the only truth that matters: our own.

The day we realize this and accept ownership for our own lives is a profound day.

While no bells, whistles, or marching bands will sound when you begin to strive for what you really want, you'll feel much joy because you'll be closer to being the person you were designed to be.

Remember, good will always be the enemy of great. Those who reject discussions about self-awareness tend to be with partners they only tolerate and with kids who don't reflect their values. For various reasons they're not inspired to make things different. They also tend to spend their time in a job where they know they're only good. Such choices inevitably take a toll on personal and professional effectiveness. Does your life reflect the choice to just exist? Or does it show you're starting to establish your visions? That you want your journey to be exciting, meaningful, and successful?

Take a chance on you. Gauge your comfort level for risk. Could you handle the worst-case scenario?

What do you stand to gain, emotionally and mentally, for taking a chance on you? How is your intuition prompting you?

How satisfied are you with knowing every day is more or less the same?

Why are you doing it? What if the next five years of your life were the same – would that be okay with you?

What if more was possible? What would you be willing to do to get it?

Figure out the list of questions you need to have satisfied and then ask yourself what you need to do next. Take some leaps of faith. Trust that the net will appear.

Put into place a strategy of living from the inside out. Expect the best. Good is not good enough for you.

WHAT ABOUT YOU?

- How clear are you on the type of journey you want to have?

- Are you someone who tends to go along to get along?

- What are the consequences of this approach for you personally?

- How does this approach affect your results?

- What do you live for?

- Women, if you married for money or ease, is it working for you in meaningful ways?

- How much effort for intimacy do either of you make with each other?

- How do you feel about that?

- What do you get for feeling anything less than positive?

- Is it worth it?

- How much do you feel valued as a person vs. for the money you bring home?

- How often are you honest with yourself? Where do you want and need to be more honest with yourself?

- How much of what you do is driven by external variables rather than because you actually believe what you claim to believe?

- Where do you think, sense, know that better returns are possible in your life?

Chapter 4

Eyes Wide Open

*People will do anything, no matter
how absurd, in order to avoid
facing their own soul.*

–Carl Jung

Y**OU** know what would happen if you
drove with your eyes closed. The same
is true of your life. If the way you get
through it is to squeeze your eyes shut
and hope for the best, you're going
to crash. The best way to live is in full
awareness, eyes wide open. Even just
beginning to acknowledge and consider
options will make you more likely to
explore new choices, which will then put
you in the position to choose a better life.

One form of closing your eyes is to
continue letting others tell you what
matters most. All that's going to get
you is *more of the same* or *more of what*

they have. Do you want either of these outcomes? You'll be empowered to realize so much more of your potential by being honest about what *is* and how satisfied you are with your results right now.

Increase Your Awareness

Just as "Location, location, location" is the mantra of real estate agents, so "Awareness, awareness, awareness" is the mantra of personal and professional development and effectiveness. It doesn't take much for you to increase your awareness of the influences in your life. I'm talking about what matters to you; what you most want and need; how satisfied you are; and where in your life you sell out on yourself. You'll start progressing just by noticing, and taking action on, what needs to change. And remember, we all share space with others who influence our perceptions and realities. What will you do if your efforts aren't appreciated? Will you stop, give up, or perhaps not even start in the first place? What could slow you down? What will you do about it?

Don't dismiss or overlook anything until you've allowed yourself to notice it and consider it. Consider what *is* and notice the things you normally dismiss. This will help you see the choices in front of you and then to improve. Notice everything, even things that don't come when/where/how you expect.

By increasing your self-awareness, you will naturally shift from being externally focused to being internally focused. When you begin to consider who you really are, your focus will shift from considering other people first to considering your own thoughts first. This will help you understand your drivers better and bring you closer to realizing greater success and being more effective for others.

If guilt or fear are holding you back from noticing and making certain choices, remind yourself that if you win, the people who love you will win, too, because you'll be happier and much good comes from that.

Your Wheel of Life

The freedom to choose doesn't mean you get to determine the categories of life. It means you decide for yourself *where* you want to focus your life and *when*, vis-à-vis those categories. The well-known Wheel of Life exercise divides these categories into eight.

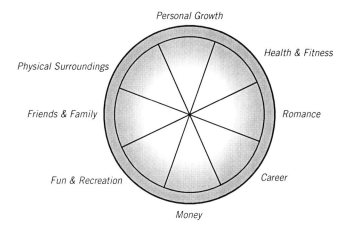

For the first year or so after I was introduced to the Wheel of Life, I scored myself based on how actively involved I was in each category. My scores were consistently high. I couldn't figure out why this exercise did so little for me. My perception changed when I finally had the courage to consider each category from the perspective of personal satisfaction. I looked through the lens of my values, asking myself to what degree they were showing up in these eight areas. Although the output wasn't always comforting, I was more at ease. I was no longer faced with the tension I felt from having high scores while still feeling unsatisfied.

In my practice, clients want to be pushed and challenged. I use the Wheel of Life to help them define aloud what each area includes and represents for them and to question their commitment levels. The process often works best when done in this edgy way with another person. See if you can find someone to do this with you.

Most of us adults don't have an outlet for honestly considering our lives, and for considering them not necessarily because something is broken and needs fixing. The Wheel of Life exercise gives you this outlet, if you're honest in how you use it.

Do this exercise throughout your journey. It is informative and provocative.

When you consider the different categories of the Wheel of Life, give yourself a score, working from the inside of the wheel to the outside, with 1 being low, 10 being high. Once you have completed the exercise, connect the dots and notice how closely the result resembles a wheel. Imagine what the ride would be like if it was a wheel on your car.

WHAT ABOUT YOU?

- *Is the journey you're on bumpy or smooth?*

- *Is it so smooth you notice yourself feeling restless, bored?*

- *Is it time to revisit the vision that got you here?*

- *Which areas of your life have you been neglecting?*

- *Consider your scores and ask yourself why you gave yourself the ratings you did in each area.*

- *How actively are you participating in your own life?*

- *How is that approach working for you?*

Feeling the Energy

All areas within the Wheel of Life matter to us and affect us, but to varying degrees. It's not realistic to maintain focus on all eight areas. If you try to do that, you won't be able to focus on what brings you the most joy and personal reward. Life sometimes requires us to limit our focus to the most pressing matters. Focusing on one or two inspiring, motivating areas at any one time will help you get through your challenges with better results.

Nothing I'm stating is news to you; you know this. I just want to remind you of what you know and to show you how increasing your self-awareness will help you be your best.

My client Leonard states that fulfillment is a luxury and being our best an unattainable notion. Not true. Life is a constant stream of choices. Either you want greatness and pursue it, or – for whatever reason – you don't. I'm just sharing my formula, experiences, and insights in the hope that you'll consider your choices more strategically as a result.

I suggest to clients that they notice the pieces of their life that interest or inspire them the most. Our natural tendency as good boys and girls is to think we have to focus on where our scores are low. Instead, consider the areas where you feel the energy. For example, if you've never cared about your physical environment, it may be because you didn't know how to care about it, or maybe you just don't care. Don't try to make yourself care. Assess the other possibilities and focus on the ones you do care about. They will bring you the best results and satisfaction – and the other ones may have to wait for another day.

Think of your own life. Your priorities shift, don't they? There may be a time when you will focus on having fun, along with your career and finances. In another chapter of your life, you may be more focused on family and friends, health and finances. And so it will go throughout your life.

It's all good and relevant. I'm not encouraging you to ignore the needs of those you care about but to be honest with yourself and the people you care about.

Desires Come First

Consider some of your more important decisions. Did you buy this house or that one? Did you marry the person everyone wanted you to marry? Did you make the career choice you really wanted to make? Perhaps you projected inward for your answers in your decision-making process, listening to your intuition, that voice inside of you, your gut. Or perhaps not. What value might there be in revisiting the processes you typically use to make your choices? Do these processes still help? Maybe they served you at that point in your life and now different things matter because you're no longer the same person. Things change. People change.

Based on my own experiences and what my clients share with me, I see that our choices don't always reflect an awareness of the objectives we want to realize. I would like to propose and offer a *new vision*, one in which we always assess and strive to understand our own wants and needs first before we consider what the outside world wants us to do. (See chapter 9 for more on new vision.)

Considering ourselves first is the scarier approach. But what if more of us stopped turning to the left or right for our answers? What if we encouraged one another to tap into our personal values of courage and boldness? The answer to that question is clear. We would be more likely to live in a world in which a greater number of us were happy with our lives. None of us wins when so many are unhappy. There's no question about it. We need a new vision.

Do you really want to continue handing down and perpetuating the same flawed mental models you've lived by to this point? Aren't you tired of the same old? Do you want your kids to live the way you've lived?

Jack has an idea of what he wants and needs in a partner, does some due diligence, and chooses Suzy for his wife. Suzy figures if the person has looks, worldly success, and is interested, he's husband-worthy.

What's happening here?

Jack, based on models handed down to him by other men and women, is choosing a person based on what he wants and needs, with little to no concern for what this other person in his life wants and needs.

Suzy is choosing based on models handed down to her regarding women's roles and responsibilities. She thinks a wealthy husband will guarantee her a great life. Her choices are an extension of her ignorance about herself.

Jack and Suzy are making their choice robotically rather than methodically.

Neither person is considering the full implications of their choice, having done only a surface due diligence that satisfies the short term. They choose to ignore the glaring elephant in the room. Suzies and Jacks hook up all the time and the results usually play out in the same ways. Lacking self-awareness, they sabotage their chances for a successful and fulfilling life together.

There's value in identifying the moments that have shaped your character, influenced your focus, and put you on the path you're on now, good or bad. These are the moments that helped you put stakes in the ground. You may have forgotten the takeaways you learned. Revisiting them may remind you of who you are.

Your Reference Points

There's a strong chance and likelihood that if you went to school, attended a place of worship, or were involved in community activities, you're holding on to reference points that may not be serving you. You may not be aware of these reference points or even agree with them – and yet still unconsciously hold on to them.

The problem is, when we do this, we become stuck without knowing why. The models were handed down, in part, to ensure that we achieved good in our lives, as measured by that good ol' status quo. There is safety, security, and comfort in good. I can speak to this model of safety. As the daughter of an immigrant, I was encouraged to focus on jobs that offered a pension. My dad wanted me to have some financial security and a predictable life.

When we make decisions for safety or security, is it because we know ourselves or because we don't and thereby are unaware of what else is possible for us?

The journeys we take are ours alone to chart; we can choose to be true to our design or not. The more we can know about our own design, the more likely we'll stop selling out on ourselves and make informed decisions.

Make your choices with your eyes wide open.

Jeremy, a client of mine, seemingly has it made. His company does very well. He is revered in his industry and makes lots of money.

With their kids out of the nest, his wife, Patty, now had more time on her hands and no sense of identity that she could leverage for herself. With their marriage over, Jeremy has health issues. The changes in his life have been unsettling to him for obvious reasons and have affected his focus, his effectiveness, and even his quality as a person. To have a sense of security, he is focusing on what he's most accustomed to: long hours at work and on the golf course.

Jeremy surrounds himself with people with lower standards so he can always feel and look superior and secure. Ego validation is important to him. This strategy is failing him and his company.

When we started our engagement, Jeremy's objective was to stay focused so he could maintain his effectiveness in negotiating mergers and acquisitions for his company. He knew he didn't want to be an eight-cylinder car and be firing on only six of them.

I share his example because he eventually kind of acknowledged to himself that the only place he has ever been an eight-cylinder car was in his head. This was tough for him to admit. He's the president of a private company and is satisfied with his good results. He doesn't want to be challenged. With his high IQ, he always feels he knows best, and he usually does. He also lacks the conviction to keep pushing.

Jeremy allowed other people's perceptions of his life to be his reality. He couldn't understand why his marriage dissolved, since he had afforded his family such a great lifestyle. He didn't see how the marriage could have been unfulfilling for his wife. In the case of his company, since he was always the same person, it wasn't easy for him to change much in his leadership approach. He knew his life and work weren't feeding his mind enough and just accepted this was what happens at certain ages and stages of life. Especially since he was doing all the right things by honoring the right models.

He had not sought integrity in his marriage, as defined by being where he truly wanted to be. He hadn't felt it necessary to address the issues. He had gone elsewhere to get his physical needs met. He has more money than he knows how to use. Plagued by his middle-class mentality, he just keeps on accumulating and saving it.

Throughout his adult years, Jeremy was overwhelmed with his own life. He had no idea of how to take his satisfaction and fulfillment to the next level. The soft stuff, and a willingness to deal with his personal reality, caused him too much discomfort. Besides, there was no time for that; he was too busy working and golfing.

Jeremy the provider – for his family and his company

– was the one who suffered most, and not in a noble way. He knew he was choosing weak actions. He was willing to go through the motions of living for the sake of the team, both the one at home and the one at work.

His mental models had told him he had to suck it up and be a family man. He continued to accept the mental models that got him into an eighteen-year incompatible relationship in the first place.

It was very unpleasant to work with Jeremy because he had no real desire to change; he just wanted to be more focused on his strategies. He had begun using women because his looks and success allowed him to. He wasn't ready to examine how slavishly he had modeled his life on external expectations. He wasn't ready to question his assumption that if he lived by enough of the right rules and denied or hid the truth about himself, everything would work out in the end.

Greatness for him is about having money because that's an easy way to gauge success. He admitted to me he was confused and wasn't proud of all his actions/choices and that he was lost. He was truly "caught between a dream and a nightmare," as the Blue Rodeo song "Sheba" puts it.

We grew his net worth. I did what the client needed me to do. I know we could have achieved even more, except Jeremy was too entrenched in his middle-class mindset to give himself permission to want more for himself.

As for Jeremy's company, it will never be more than a tier two company because he lacks the courage to do the things he could do. Jeremy did come to admit that good was good enough for him. He continues to use his talent for strategic thinking to ensure goodness rather than greatness.

Personal growth varies from individual to individual. Though Jeremy seems unlikely to grow, the seeds of possibility have been planted. They may germinate for him one day.

Success comes when we choose based on intuition rather than instinct or protocol. The more options we're open to *seeing*, the more open-ended our future. The standard we can choose to embrace is win/win, when both parties, company or partner, are where they want to be and are happy as a result. If that's not your reality, explore how it could be, or move on. There's no harm in using your eyes to see, or in using your feelings to gauge your level of satisfaction. Surely that's why God gave us eyes and feelings.

Even if you can't see the possibilities or options now, they're there. Your values, including the value of courage, will enable you to find them.

The Need to Challenge

Very little makes immediate sense to me. For too many years in my short life, I have had to find my own way. I've learned to be a sponge when around people who can help me learn what I don't understand. But who knows how to access the other stuff, the less concrete information we only sense we have? It would be so much easier if there were a magic wand to make living easier. There is, however, a magical way to get closer to the truth of who you are, one that requires courage, focus, and effort.

Challenge everything rather than just trust things are the way they are for a reason. Consider challenging more of your processes and examining more of the models you're shaping your life on. Do you even know what you're hoping to achieve by following the staid models? If you're following the steps of those models, how are the results working for you?

The willingness to see is what empowers us to realize more of our potential. The "going along to get along" approach can work for those who have no concrete objectives of their own. However, we were all created to be ourselves. I hope it's only a matter of time before you realize this and start to feel an active sense of dis-ease. Be thankful for this feeling because it gives you a chance to reconsider your approach.

Who wants to live a life of selling out on themselves?

If you've been letting society dictate the choices available to you, chances are you're trying to find more with no real options to choose from. You may become a workaholic; obsess over the kids and make them your life; allow yourself to be labeled by society as having a mid-life crisis (regardless of your age); lose your health; live an empty life; get a lover or make golf your mistress; or live in deception to yourself and those around you, or, or, or ...

It's always useful to challenge your own processes and rationale, because things change. Other people's input can be valuable, when it is. Perspective is always something to consider.

What do you stand to gain by being your own person, focusing your time and energy in pursuits that give you more joy for living? What do you stand to lose?

The Self-Knowledge Economy

It's generally accepted that we're living in a knowledge economy. Fritz Machlup, an Austrian-American economist who died 1983, was among the first to examine knowledge as an economic resource. Peter Drucker popularized the concept in his books *The Effective Executive* (1966) and *The Age of Discontinuity: Guidelines to Our Changing Society* (1969).

Drucker distinguishes between two types of workers: manual workers who work with their hands to produce goods or services and knowledge workers who work with their head and produce ideas, knowledge, and information.

I have a different take on this. I believe we live in a *self-knowledge* economy. The most important kind of knowledge is self-knowledge. Self-knowledge workers are the most successful people personally and in their work. Strategies that incorporate *true knowledge of self* consistently net greater results and satisfaction. Self-knowledge is the oil that makes life's wheels run smoother.

That phrase "true knowledge of self" is useful in its lack of specificity, because life forces us to start with broad strokes. When we consider the full scope of an opportunity, including the implications to the self, we will make better decisions. It's crazy how this works, but it does!

In a self-knowledge economy, the most strategic investment for an organization, team, or individual is in-depth awareness of the person or people involved. Companies and individuals who make this investment can expect greater results and success, because people are predictable.

So if you're not seeing the results you want, reassess your plan, refocus, and respond by increasing your self-awareness and understanding. This kind of knowledge will make it easier for you to troubleshoot and make better contributions to your organization, family, and community. Take the time, having established your own personal awareness, to know more about the other personalities joining you around the strategic planning table of your life or business. What good is knowing what makes you tick if you don't consider what makes others tick? The people around you have a bearing on your results.

To grow more, question everything. Be open to considering what more is available to you and within you. As you then decide on the kind of life you really want to lead, be more vigilant about the choices you make. Always choose what you really want and need.

What you choose for your life is yours to choose. Your individual journey can look as diverse, broad, or grand as you want it to be. You decide. The possibilities available to you are endless because you'll never reach your limits, even if you think you have.

WHAT ABOUT YOU?

- *How did you choose the journey you're on?*

- *What vision were you pursuing?*

- *What drives you now?*

- *What most influenced your choices? The people around you, recordings you heard growing up, a teacher, someone you were trying to impress or emulate?*

- *Alone with this book now, ask yourself how truly satisfied you are with where your journey has brought you at this point in your life.*

- *Try not to answer that question by looking only at the toys around you or your house or salary. Look inside to where only you exist.*

- *How proud are you of yourself?*

- *How clearly do you know what within you is responsible for where you are, good or bad?*

- *When will you start making better choices, or when will you start being more consistent?*

- *Has your life been too focused?*

- *Have you been an active enough participant in your own life?*

- *Considering the entirety of your life, in what areas do you notice you tend to settle too quickly?*

Part 2

Focus

$$\frac{\textit{Self-Awareness}}{\begin{array}{l} + \qquad \textbf{\textit{Focus}} \\ + \qquad \textit{Strategy} \end{array}}$$

$$= \textbf{\textit{SUCCESS}}$$

Chapter 5

Values Are Everything

*You cannot escape the results
of your thoughts. Whatever your
present environment may be, you
will fall, remain or rise with your
thoughts, your vision, your ideal.
You will become as small as your
controlling desire; as great as your
dominant aspiration.*

–James Allen

THIS world is best suited to those who
are willing to engage with the process
of their own lives. Another way to say
"engage with" is "focus on." Focus is
the second part of my success formula
and is the topic of this part of the book.
Focus is defined as the concentration

of attention or energy on something. Many of us have set SMART goals – you know, goals that are specific, measurable, attainable, realistic, and timely. I'm not talking about that sort of thing. I'm talking about the kind of focus that comes from being truly interested in a pursuit, not because we have to or because we feel we should but because the objects of our focus are meaningful, exciting, and motivating for us.

While self-awareness, the topic of the first part of this book, is critical, it's not enough. To achieve any level of excellence in life, we must learn to master the mindset of focus. We all know, intellectually, that this kind of focus enables us to concentrate and complete tasks to a higher degree. The better we can concentrate, the stronger our brains become. With stronger brains we learn new things faster and more effectively and experience more of life. Focus is a huge factor in realizing success. Focus helps us change *trying* into *doing*. As Yoda, the great Jedi Master, said to Luke Skywalker, "Do or do not; there is no *try*."

Focus, in its action orientation, creates results. This may seem counterintuitive because being focused doesn't always translate immediately into visible action. However, as we make choices in order to get focused, we get clearer on what really matters and are better poised to consider what jives with who we are. This knowledge enables us to be more strategic in our efforts, focus, and resources. And that helps us achieve the kind of results we desire.

How much focus have you put on your own fascinating design? Lead with a focus on who you are, just as an experiment, and notice what happens. Are any of your results different for it? For example, if you know your preferences, assert in favor of them versus what the others want you to do. Do not assert to be a wet blanket; assert because they are what brings you happiness. You'll feel good, even when the choices do not play out the way you hoped. Focusing on who you are enables you to bring more of your strengths, more of you, into your actions. That way you'll be on your way to different and better results, professionally and personally.

What You Focus On

Focus requires a clear and uncluttered mind. That's a challenge nowadays. More than ever in history, we live in a world of distractions. There are so many demands for our attention and time, so many inducements to stray from what we're seeking to achieve.

Undeterred focus always results in success. Just ask Peter Munk of Barrick Gold or Roberto Luongo of the Vancouver Canucks. Both men experience losses. They always rise again. Why? Because of luck? No – because they understand their strengths.

While it's clear how focused energy translates into great returns, it's not so clear where and how to best focus our energy. There's a risk, therefore, that we'll focus on the wrong things. Yet risk we must. Give yourself a chance to focus your talent in the ways that help you feel most alive.

You may be in a role, whether personally or professionally, that does not incorporate or factor in your key values and motivators. If you're not aligned with your role, you won't create valuable results.

That's why your focus is best directed at increasing your levels of self-awareness before you get too busy with much else. There can be no more useful and relevant truth than who you are. When you're empowered with full awareness of your personal truths, and you include the other truths around you, nothing can stop you – you can walk on water. As Carl Jung is said to have celebrated with a plaque on his wall, "Invoked or not invoked, God is present. Called or not called, the god will be there."

Values and Feelings

Values were mentioned in our discussion of self-awareness in the first part of this book. Let's focus more tightly on them now.

I've heard there are always two wills available to us at any point: permissive will and perfect will. The former is about doing whatever we want, however we want. The latter is about trusting in ourselves, listening to our soul and being open to being guided. Perfect will always seemed so inviting to me, but I liked being able to control life and make things happen. My approach made it very difficult for me to be open to seeing what could be perfect for me. I was always aware of my intuition telling me to trust more but that seemed nebulous; control was easier because it was visible through action.

Trusting requires us to access our feelings. Feelings never held any real pull for me, though. When I did finally decide to go there, it was easier to understand my dis-ease and my feelings. It was liberating when I gave myself permission to just *feel*, without demanding a logical reason to feel, and not requiring other people's approval to validate my feeling. This approach freed me from the guilt I felt about feeling unsatisfied when my checklist of needs was being met. Things got a lot easier when I removed guilt from my shoulders; I felt lighter and ready to focus more on my life.

Here's the key: We find our true values by focusing on our feelings.

In my case, I knew I was not feeling **excited** about my life. I wanted to be **inspired** by my pursuits. I knew when I pursued **challenging, meaningful** objectives which had an element of **adventure/risk**, I was **engaged, motivated,** and **excited** about feeling alive. I knew I enjoyed being **intense** and **bold** – that the bolder I could be, the more open I was to **learning** new things and the more **invigorated** I felt.

I knew I loved what my **creativity** enabled. I loved how

my horizons expanded when I brought in creativity. I knew it was my **faith** in God that gave me the **courage** to *be* who he designed me to be, always pushing past the limits of what I accepted as good.

I also knew I was never sincerely satisfied when my actions were dictated by what or how others wanted me to be. My effectiveness, satisfaction, potential, and influence all increased when I did what I believed in. **Integrity**, which is about believing in what you're doing, is a bitch of a value to honor. Yet it's my chief guiding value; it's how I find **truth** in my life.

I saw how I am **curious** about things and want to have the **freedom** to explore my thoughts and go where I feel directed. I want the freedom to increase my understanding and actively **grow** in body/mind/soul.

I value **intimacy** and need to be surrounded by kindred souls – by **stimulating** people with whom meaningful friendships evolve. I engage only in friendships, professional or personal, in which there is depth, substance, and stimulation, where real growth is afforded. I need **fun** in my life.

The most exciting value I lead with is **possibility**. This value can transform every situation, moment, and relationship into an **adventure full of challenge**.

These are some of the top values I seek to have satisfied in my pursuits and relationships so I feel alive and motivated. It's not that I have to have all of these values all of the time; it's that I know I'm most alive when I honor as many of them as possible. I'm an action-oriented person and these values are both about my being and my doing. As I continue in my evolution, I'm also learning about the power of **compassion**. Compassion is easy for me to give and not so easy for me to accept, yet I know it's a loving value and action that can enable much.

I'm excited to observe my own growth. I value the beauty associated with life more and more: how poetic much of life is, and how much joy I feel in being my children's mother. These feelings are not easy for me to understand. I did not grow up this way. Yet my soul longs to have these feelings/ needs met.

The more we can acknowledge the needs of our souls, the more fulfilled, happy, and excellent we will be. I'm open to considering values that come from outside my reference points because I sense they'll help me understand the most powerful value of all: *love*.

The process of knowing and having the values we do does not place our needs and values ahead of everything and everyone else. Our values are reference points we can trust to help us know how and where to focus for more success, more enjoyment, and more personal satisfaction. We either consider a new approach for different and better results, or we don't. The choice is only ours to make. However, we have everything to gain when we choose in favor of our essence.

Most people are living their values already, just not consciously. My point is that the more consciously we live our values, the better and more consistent our results and our joy.

The Values Mandate

Knowing my values and other people's values helps me understand why people act in certain ways. I now know to look at the values at play when communication is not easy.

There's no value in judging your values; they just *are*, so get to know them. I have no idea where some of my key values come from and that's okay – in fact, that makes it even more exciting for me because it helps me understand how they're a function of me from birth.

Values are the spiritual DNA God gives us to help us realize our visions. When we honor these values, in whatever forms they actively take, and focus our lives on them, we will live successful lives. This is the one mandate he has given us for our lives; it's our choice whether to accept it or not.

Will you successfully fulfill your mandate for life?

WHAT ABOUT YOU?

- *If you're not clear on your values and think this is limiting you, it isn't; it's just slowing you down. You're probably living many of your values without having labeled them as values. Which values would you fiercely defend?*

- *How often do you not assert after your values/feelings?*

- *Consider the things you do that bring you the most joy.*

- *What do you need and seek in order to be stimulated?*

- *What do you most enjoy doing? What else?*

- *Keep going, and with each answer, ask yourself how that makes you feel. Whatever feelings you identify, note them; record them in your journal after your notes from the Wheel of Life exercise. (See chapter 4.)*

- *What actions were present when you achieved your most fulfilling triumphs? Resist the temptation to focus solely on the tangible triumphs.*

- *Consider your defining moments – the toughest decisions you have had to make.*

- *Why were you making those decisions?*

- *What feelings were you seeking to realize?*

- *Did you realize what you were seeking?*

- *What else did you get out of these moments?*

Your Must-Have Values

It's time for you to come up with a list of your top ten must-have values.

Think back to times when you didn't realize the success you were seeking. What was missing that may have helped you achieve better success? If this involves a relationship, consider the *feeling* the person enables in you or brings out in you.

Consider what made one of your worst moments so bad. What specific feeling did that prompt? What feelings or values were you forced to sacrifice? How important are those values to you now? Note that guilt is not a value. We're not naturally hardwired to feel guilty; guilt is a form of manipulation that comes as a result of not kowtowing to other people's agendas.

You may be living many of your values already. If you claim them and recognize how critical they are to your effectiveness as a human being, like food and water are to your physical body, then you'll honor them and they'll be present in more of your life. When you lead with your values, you'll have better results, because your values are like your instruction book for a successful life. This makes sense. Your weed whacker is great for weeding and useless as a dishwasher. Be yourself and you'll work better.

If you notice family brings with it some great feelings that you cherish and want more of, it's safe to say family is a strong value for you. If you notice you enjoy being part of a team or group of people, then community may well be a major need in your life. If you notice you get bored unless you're being creative, honor the value of creativity in every aspect of your life.

Consider all of your values, even what makes you cry when you see a movie. Why are you crying? What's the feeling about? Do you want more of it, or does it lead you to discover a value that's meaningful for you, one you might not be acknowledging enough? The more time you spend in this exploration, the better you'll understand what drives you to be excellent. The more must-have values you can be clear on, the better. Some of the values you identify you may only enjoy. You may not need them that much in your life. Get clear on the values you *must have* and consider how you could bring more of them into your life.

By knowing your key values, you'll be less likely to get sucked into things that don't honor you and what you desire in order to be great. Let your values become your standard for engagement. Be more selective in what and with whom you engage. Being more intentional with your choices will take you from good to great.

Mothering can be a challenge for me because I didn't grow up learning womanly things. Domestic excellence doesn't show up on my values radar either. I would much rather hang out with my kids. Knowing this about myself led me to engage live-in caregivers. Creativity, resourcefulness, and my need for efficiency all supported this decision. It enables me to direct my time to where there's more return on effort and results for my kids and me. My relationship with the kids is the stronger for it. They understand why this is my choice. It shows them we're in choice and need to be gentle with ourselves and be creative when dealing with challenges.

Identifying your key values isn't an optional exercise. Values are what put the kick into everything you do. You can influence the degree of satisfaction you have in your life just by taking the time to know what defines you from the inside because with this knowledge you can choose more intelligently.

You may end up identifying more than ten top values, and that's great. Bottom line: The more these values show up in how you live your life, the more excellence you'll have.

Honoring Your Values

Okay, so to bring values like nurturing to your corporate role isn't going to help you be more successful per se. However, if you have these "less business-like" types of values and want to lead with them more, consider industries or roles that are more susceptible to nurturing.

Parenting is a job option if that's what satisfies your key values. Just be prepared for when it doesn't or when it stops being enough.

If your values do not line up with what you're doing and you think that's fine because no one's complaining about your work, that's okay. It's safe to say, however, that you're only good at your job. If you value integrity and need to believe in what you believe, then you're being called to move past *good* to *great*. Give yourself and your role the chance for better results. Otherwise you're in a lose/lose situation. Who goes through life choosing that?

Honoring only a few of your top ten values is good, and honoring as many on your list as possible is *great*. There is and always will be a correlation between your success and your ability to realize your main values. Trying to make yourself value something you don't value will only add to the stress in your life. Similarly, another person can't dictate what you value. The values and actions dictated by other people are "shoulds." When another person or a group thinks you should do something, that doesn't mean you must. Instead, seek excellence for yourself; it doesn't take that much more effort – just focused effort.

If you value love and yet your actions do not bring you love, look inward and ask yourself how much you love *you*. When you love yourself, you're empowered to love and be loved by others who share your values and are able to appreciate who you are as you are. New actions aren't always easy to incorporate because life gets busy. One of the best ways to produce sustainable change is by remaining open to being held accountable. Monitor how attentive you are with each step you take, to who you really are.

You're so much more than who you have been. It's easy for us to get our ladders on the wrong wall and consider our lives from only one value or perspective. If you value nurturing, do not make your life only about that and still expect interesting people to be drawn to you. Unless, that is, you don't value or need interesting people as long as you're able to nurture. Just be fair to yourself and those around you. Don't hold it against your partner or others if they don't value what you value. Surround yourself with enough people who do, so you, too, are valued rather than taken for granted.

For illustrative purposes, nurturing could be replaced by any value. For example, if your partner is a workaholic and loves achieving tangible results, recognize that she must be true to her design. If you can't handle the value, that's your issue, not hers. There are people for everyone; finding the right people takes effort just like anything else worth having.

Rob is a good example of getting in touch with values that may actually lead one away from business life. He and I began working together after he had been downsized from his old job as a senior sales executive. He wanted me to focus with him on finding work outside the field of sales that would still replace his income. He said he was surprised by his visceral reaction to the idea of going back into sales. He said he felt as if he was slamming on the brakes.

He spoke of his emotional response to his old work and that led us to his values.

It quickly became clear he had never felt much passion for making money in sales. He was saying all the right words but the noise between us made it difficult for me to understand his words. He seemed a bit hopeless because he couldn't come up with a line of work that would spark passion in him.

I asked him about past pursuits that had summoned up feelings of passion. Rob came alive when he talked about music. He had a degree in composition and had made a promising start as a pianist before setting it all aside to become the responsible husband and father. He did what he had to do. He was shocked when he put words on what he had lost by abandoning music. Our talks inspired him to carve out space in his house for a music room, start working on some new compositions, and put out an ad for fellow musicians interested in contemporary composition. His ad was answered, and he even ended up forming an ensemble.

He was surprised how much energy this gave him to find other things that jazzed him. He ended up taking a course that allowed him to pursue a leadership role in the music industry. I asked him how he felt about doing the part of his new job that still involved sales. He just laughed and said, "Selling something I care about reminds me how much I enjoy sales."

His efforts are now bringing him joy, not sadness.

There are many Robs out there. I often discover a disconnect in my clients between what they tell me they enjoy and how much of it actually shows up in their lives. Is it any wonder people focus only on the kids, work longer hours than they need to, or golf as much as they do? It's safe to say that when we fake it, there ain't a whole lot of fulfillment or results going on. The people who do realize gains on the backs of other people may be happy; the people who went along to get along are often left feeling empty and bored. A nice win/lose!

Going along to get along can work for those whose values are **other-centric**. If values such as **nobility** and **selflessness** are important to you, then stay focused on others. If such values don't drive you, then consider finding the ones that do and live according to them. There's no honor in making others or family your focus if what you're really doing is avoiding the search for your own drivers.

Our personal values are our road map through the seasons of our life. Knowing them and honoring them increases our effectiveness as leaders and as citizens of the world. Values are what define us and give us our unique identities. Knowing and living according to *our* core values also makes it easier for us to make decisions. Stop being passive in any part of your life. There's so much more inside you and out there for you.

The Value of Integrity

Knowing your values is huge, and still not enough. The real power lies in *claiming* your values by living them. Awareness and application of your values gives you a strategic advantage, enabling you to win on your terms in all of your roles.

This is where the value of **integrity** comes in. Unfortunately, the word tends to be thrown around indiscriminately. It's part of most mission and vision statements out there. People who are living scummy lives boast of high integrity. People who don't lead with conviction say they're living with integrity. Yes, it's possible to be a good person even if you do not lead with conviction about anything, and there's a place in this world for all of us, and that is not integrity. Integrity demands conviction. Being nice doesn't mean you're leading with integrity; it just means you're being nice.

Integrity in its truest sense forms the basis of who we are; it's what binds together everything we believe and value. When integrity is present we lead with conviction; we honor our design and what we sincerely value. Who but other boring people can enjoy the company of someone who lacks conviction? There are those to whom conviction is irrelevant. They have chosen to hang their hats on surface values focused on *doing* rather than *being*. They may be thrill seekers, career climbers, great intellects, or traditionalists. These types surround themselves with others like them and focus on thrills, money, ego pursuits, and the status quo.

Value Clashes

Go back to the list you built of your top ten values. Now cross-reference your values with your Wheel of Life scores. How often do your must-have values show up in each area? What do you need to be doing more of, or differently, so more of them are present and you are more satisfied?

Consider making **integrity** one of your must-haves and direct it to whatever you want, however you choose. This isn't necessarily an invitation for your intellect to evaluate; give **courage** a chance to be in charge.

Value clashes like this happen often. **Intellect** and **courage** may both number among your top values, challenging you to choose which you value more. One way to prioritize your values, when values clash, is to consider which value, when you pursue it, brings you more fulfillment. There's no right or wrong, and only you know. Sometimes it may be one. Sometimes it may be the other.

If you choose to allow **integrity** to weigh-in, then you may want to consider a policy of *not* engaging in an activity unless your values like intellect and/or courage are required or present.

And so it goes with any of the values that inspire you most. Decide how you want to use your values to inform the way you live your life. It may be worthwhile for you to consider each value individually, asking yourself how each one could better inform your choices.

When we choose based on our desires and feelings, and not driven primarily by need, we will become stronger in our sense of self. It's not easy. Nothing worth having *is*. Allow everything to be open to challenge.

The Values of Faith and Courage

Two other values that will serve you as you define and develop yourself are **faith** and **courage**. Consider including these values, along with **integrity**, on your list of must-haves. Revere these three values. They're truly powerful. Magic will happen when you incorporate them into your pursuits. These values have to resonate for you, though. I won't take it personally if they don't inspire you. Find the ones that do. I just want you to succeed.

If you honor these three values, nothing can stop you from realizing your vision. Unless, of course, you want to be stopped – but not very many people whose eyes are wide open begin pursuits they don't really care about.

This book is about my formula for *more* success; my mission is to let you know there's another way through this life and it's one where you are in more control of your own life. Following my formula will bring you more success, whether financially, mentally, spiritually, or all of the above. Becoming more aware of yourself and focusing on your values will take time and effort. Just get started and ask yourself deeper questions that acknowledge your feelings. The more time and effort you commit, the better and more fulfilling your results will be.

Claiming our top ten values takes the effort out of life because they help us focus on being excellent. We're not meant to have lives of struggle. How could that ever have been the plan? We create our own struggle in spite of having the information and tools we need to overcome our challenges. Free will dictates that we can choose to use the tools in our toolbox or keep on struggling.

Reach for your values if want better results, including a more joyous and fulfilling life. That kind of life is possible when you honor your values, even when doing so is hard. In fact, discomfort doesn't mean you're going the wrong way;

it just means you're working a new muscle. Integrity is about doing only what you believe in. The only way to grow is to step outside of your comfort zones. If you have not lived your life by values, be prepared for the discomfort that doing so inevitably causes.

Focusing on the values inherent to your design changes your journey from random to intentional. You'll be living closer to your vision – and the way I see it, closer to the vision God had for you when he created you.

Faith and Risk-Taking

We all have, to some degree, the ability to risk in favor of results. Everything we do, from baking a cake to choosing a tie to deciding our partners and what to teach our kids, involves risks of some kind. Sometimes our choices work; sometimes they don't. This can make it intimidating to take new risks, unless we remind ourselves on a regular basis of what the choice is otherwise. Either we assert what we want and believe in, or we put ourselves at the mercy of what others want. We'll be enlisted to help others reach *their* visions. Choices will always boil down to yours or theirs. Which will it be for you?

Those of you who are risk averse, who are less comfortable with the idea of taking risks – what if you focused on eliminating as many of the unknown variables that make things look risky as you can and then acted? It's okay to not approach risk head-on; allot time in your strategy to ensure that your key concerns are addressed so you can act. Knowing yourself and accepting who you are will allow you to develop better strategies for reaching your objectives. Self-awareness will enable you to see more possibilities and sets you up to win.

I don't value risk for risk's sake. I value *strategic* risk concerning what matters most to my kids and me. Valuing risk-taking helps me feel better and live better. When I take a risk, I do so knowing what I'm prepared to lose in order to gain. And I try to be as clear as I can on exactly what the risk is. Who knows if anything will be lost, or how great the gains for doing so could be? Remember, God favors risk-takers. He took a risk in creating each of us. When we live our values, our lives are more fulfilling. What's the risk to you in that approach?

WHAT ABOUT YOU?

- *What holds you back from acknowledging more of your key values?*

- *What are you afraid of?*

- *What's the biggest risk in claiming your values more actively?*

- *What's the biggest risk if you do nothing?*

- *Which of the two opportunities – the cost or the benefit – inspires you more?*

Chapter 6

Living with Conviction

*One of the truest tests
of integrity is its
blunt refusal
to be compromised.*

–Chinua Achebe

THE better we know, claim, and own our values, the better we set ourselves up for success. The next piece of the puzzle is using our focus to *action* our values with conviction.

Applying our values is not always easy. Many of us choose to keep our values private. That's okay. Our values are ours alone. We don't have to do anything with them. However, living our values with conviction means being willing to assert and communicate them.

The value of integrity requires us not only to have values but also to act according to them.

Values in Action

I use focus to help me say yes only to activities that align with my values. Of course I do engage in *some* activities not directly related to my values list. For example, I volunteer often and regularly at my kids' school and in their classes. This satisfies a different set of my values. I stray from my main values only in moderation, though. Otherwise my must-haves will be swamped by my nice-to-haves and I'll be living my life more for others than myself. Not a recipe for fulfillment. If I engage in something that's not directly linked to my values, I may incorporate my creativity to see how I can make it more stimulating for me and bring more of my values into the moment. This approach is effective only in chunks; it's not a good long-term strategy.

When I focus more on the experiences/feelings/values I must have and make decisions based on them, I achieve better results: more fun, greater self-satisfaction, and a deeper peace of mind. I'm a better person and mother for it.

Go back to the list of your top ten values (see previous chapter) and divide your list under the headings of *must-have values* and *nice-to-have values*. If you desire only a little bit of fun in your life, then fun is not a must-have. If you know you want to have compassion or family in your life, then make all of your choices accordingly so this must-have value is always active and present in your life.

For example, I value boldness, in me and others. I want my thoughts and actions to reflect this in respectful ways. Boldness is a value, not a need. Needs are about existing. I need to have food to live. Without boldness, I will not perish. However, with boldness, I will live more fully, enabled to flourish in the ways I was designed to flourish. Boldness for me is about a feeling, a desire, and a mindset fueled by possibilities. Consider what you want to feel in your life. Don't dismiss anything. It all influences the quality of your existence and is only yours to choose.

A senior executive I worked with for several years once told me, "There are two types of fighter pilots in the world: old fighter pilots and bold fighter pilots – and there are never old and bold fighter pilots." Which kind of fighter pilot do *you* want to be? What actions would you have to change to reflect your choice?

There's no wrong way to develop true knowledge of self because it all comes from you. We're all naturally hardwired to live with integrity, and integrity means taking action on our must-have values, standing up for what we believe in, not through repetitive arguments but through better results steeped in integrity.

No one wins if you're just faking it or pretending, or being unfair or unkind to people because you fooled them into thinking you believe something you don't or are someone you're not. Stop playing that game. Engage only in activities you can be in integrity to. Everyone wins then.

For example, if you love family, then put your self-awareness to active use and marry a family person – not a person who says the right words about family but one who is truly kind to their family. Don't get sucked into the stories that seek to justify why a value is not present. Be more critical than that. When we value something, things in our life will line up with that value. Let's say physical intimacy is super important to you. Pay attention, then, to compatibility in this area; otherwise it will only be a matter of time before something has to give – and no one wins.

Always be vigilant and live by standards, even if they're shallow ones. Just honor who you are. If you love golf, marry a golf enthusiast and you'll have a better union and a more enjoyable life. If you're a health enthusiast, show some integrity to that and be with someone who cares about health, not with a smoker or a boozer. Going against your core values will create stress and sadness in your life.

Personality Traits and Values

Each of us has a unique set of personality traits that flow from our values. For example, some of us have the trait of being big picture in our thinking. I'm not surprised, when I'm working with such clients, to find that exploration is one of their key values.

A big part of your focused self-awareness is knowing yourself, knowing the strengths and challenges associated with being who you are. It's critical for you to know the intensity of your traits because you might marry someone or take a job because you see your trait being honored, only to discover it's barely valued and/or purely situational. It will always be tough for you to justify your wants when big choices are in front of you, but do it. Play to win in your life. Sharks grow to the size of their tank. Are you satisfied with a fish tank or do you need an ocean to swim in? Don't think it doesn't matter; it does. Make all of your choices based on how they enable you to be the best you can be, how they "enable you to enable" others to reach their destiny. Life is too short to limit one another, or to hold ourselves back. Who wants that on their conscience?

The land of milk and honey is ours when we live by the desires life has instilled in us. Hurtful pursuits, if they show lack of concern for another, can't be masked as a value. The land of milk and honey awaits us all; we just have to claim our values and we are there.

The Evolutionary Option

You know what you've got and how well it's working, so why not consider a new option, too? Evolution works only in forward motion, whether we can see it or not. We're designed to advance. What do you have to lose by moving forward? And even if you do lose something, it will only be for the short term, because evolution does not work backwards.

Instead of focusing on possible negative consequences, remember the gains that are possible for you just by being in greater integrity to yourself. There's always a cost when you stand up for something. It may be a hit to your pride and self-confidence or to your finances and reputation. Whatever it is, it's short term and will pass. Besides, if you believe strongly in or about something and *do not* honor that belief, you'll still take a hit to your pride, even if you're the only one who knows about it.

When we lead with conviction, we experience more benefits than negative consequences. Nothing in this book promises your questions will stop when you live in greater integrity. In fact, the process is like peeling an onion: Each new choice made with integrity will reveal another layer and you'll probably have even more questions. Don't fear them; engage your curiosity and deal with whatever you come up with. Otherwise it's kind of like all those things in your basement or garage. Unused values just add to the clutter inside you, taking up space for something new.

If we're to advance to and meet the next evolutionary opportunity and challenge for our lives, we must first successfully satisfy the opportunity and challenge before us now. Living up to our potential is based on our effective acquisition of knowledge at all levels: body, mind, and soul.

Live this way and you'll take your place among the fittest.

What Do You Believe In?

I meet many people who talk a big storm. They're amazingly brilliant and insightful when it comes to matters of the mind in business. At first I thought they were the only kind of leaders who could produce sustainable changes in themselves and the world. Now, though, after working for a decade with people in all types of leadership roles, I have no more such illusions.

The difference between those who change and those who don't is not first of all their position and how brilliantly they *think*; it's their mindset based on what they *believe* and their *convictions* to their values.

Be honest with yourself and acknowledge when/where/how you give away your energy, allow it to be taken from you, or forget who you are. Look first at your role in allowing this ownership to be taken from you and *do something* about it. Yes, sometimes we must tolerate this for the sake of the bigger picture and/or cause. The key for you is to identify whether this is an exception in your life or is actually the norm and you're just in denial about it and justifying it. If the latter, acknowledge to yourself what you're afraid of. Self-awareness is about truth and honesty about what *is* and who you are.

None of us asked to be here, and yet here we are, in a big, beautiful world with infinite possibilities. We get to choose how we want our experience to be. The world exists for us to discover it, know it, and add to it. We, too, are big and beautiful with so much potential. All we have to do is tap whichever values lead us forward to discovery, growth, success, and inner peace and joy. *It's possible to have it all.* That's my secret.

Stephanie had everything going for her: creativity, imagination, intelligence, skills, looks, and great contacts. She knew what she wanted and was determined to go after it, but her plans kept getting derailed because she was living paycheck to paycheck. She could never afford the extra time to focus on writing her book, or the extra money to hire a good editor, or an expert to help her build her Internet presence. She was caught in her own poor and powerless story, feeling sorry, feeling frustrated, but not moving forward.

A colleague suggested Stephanie work with me. I was impressed that she asked me, right from our very first session, to call her on any behaviors that were sabotaging her efforts.

In our work together, she began to see her fear of not being a publishable writer was what prompted her to be involved in activities that kept her from her writing. She was strapped financially because she used shopping to help her avoid that blank screen on her computer.

Without her "poor me" story to rely on, Stephanie had to confront some of the deeper fears she had about really going after what she wanted. Over time, she developed the courage to move forward with compassion for her fears while resolving not to let them determine her results.

Do You Believe What You Believe?

The deeper question is *whether you believe what you believe.*

If you do, and you engage only in what you believe in, you'll naturally do more due diligence in all areas of your life and you'll realize greater success. Achieving success is effortless when you're in this state of engagement. Stop driving with one eye closed; pay more attention to where your current road is taking you.

This applies to both your personal and professional life. I find this distinction somewhat artificial. Personal focusing results in better professional results, no matter how you slice it. If you're good now but you're overweight, unhappy, and struggling in body, mind, or soul, or all three, imagine just how great your life could be if you did nothing more than

turn inward for your strategy, even if the only thing that
changed was your personal satisfaction.

What do you wish you understood more about yourself
and the results you're achieving? Write a list.

What surprises you about your list?

Don't judge anything on your list; instead, consider
the various ways you can address, right now, what you've
written. Consider the experiences, emotions, and feelings
you want more of. They may include the following:

- Tranquility
- Peacefulness
- Adventure
- Stimulation
- Learning
- Fun
- Compassion
- Freedom
- Community
- Integrity
- Justice
- Excitement
- Growth
- Passion
- Service

These are just to give you an idea of how your needs may
be packaged.

As St. Augustine bottom-lines it: "Do you wish to be great?
Then begin by being. The higher your structure is to be, the
deeper must be its foundation." The higher your dreams,
aspirations, and vision for your life, the deeper your understanding must be of your strengths and limitations, and of
the values that put a spring in your step.

Purpose, Identity, and Values

People generally define their *purpose* based on the roles they have accepted for their lives. *Identity* is harder to define. That's why so many people link it to their roles, too. Identifying ourselves with our roles is externally driven, however. Our true identity is a function of our values. The alignment of our identity to these values is internally dictated and driven. When we can be clear about the values we most want to live by, we can start to claim our identity in a meaningful and sincere way.

Don't be "the hairdresser with the worst hair." Reach alignment between your identity and values and your choice of role.

Consider your situation, even if it's not where/how you want it to be. Focus on who you are and who you want to be. Be the change you want to see in the world. Stop perpetuating insincere and ineffectual patterns. Kids don't accept the "Do as I say, not as I do" approach. Believe in what you say *and* do. Explain and teach that!

Do yourself a favor. Go back to your Wheel of Life (see chapter 4) and ask yourself if you believe what you believe given how you're handling each area of your life.

This is a chance for you to consider, journal, or dialogue with someone who knows *you*. Be careful not to choose someone who will focus on the actions you've taken or the choices you've made. This person may brand you, pigeonhole you, and grant you little wiggle room. Engage someone who wants to understand what drove you to take those actions and make those choices. Be open to being challenged about your current approach and mindset.

Experiences change and shape us. The GPS of your life may need to recalculate as you find the roads you really want to take on the way to personal fulfillment.

WHAT ABOUT YOU?

- *Where in your life are you living with integrity, believing in what you believe?*

- *What are you tolerating?*

- *Are you satisfied with how much integrity you show?*

- *Where is integrity lacking in your life?*

- *Where could more integrity in your life change the quality of your life?*

- *What's the risk associated with living with more integrity?*

- *Can you handle the consequences of standing up for something?*

- *What will you lose?*

- *What will you gain?*

- *Which one matters more to you?*

Chapter 7
Values at Work

*Just as your car runs
more smoothly and requires
less energy to go faster and
farther when the wheels are in
perfect alignment, you perform
better when your thoughts,
feelings, emotions, goals, and
values are in balance.*

–Brian Tracy

W**E** began exploring the alignment
of our values and our actions in the
previous chapter. Let's drill down deeper
now to consider the alignment of our
identity with our role. You can take much
of what I say in this chapter as applying
to you personally or in your role as a
leader in the world.

Misalignment

I'm constantly surprised by how much *misalignment* there is between the roles people occupy in the workplace and their natural effectiveness based on their values and personality. As an executive coach, I can tell you it's not unusual to find right-handed executives in left-handed roles. These men and women are effective enough – in the same way that good is the enemy of great.

Leaders generally need to stay high-level. They expect or assume the right people are in the right seats. Unfortunately, as empirical evidence shows, this all too often is not the case. Some engineers *don't* have a penchant for details. Some accountants *don't* care about how the beans line up; they may be a better fit in the marketing department, given their natural sense of urgency and openness to shifting the boundary lines to reach results. And some salespeople care less about results than relationships.

First it was Mr. Anderson, my grade eight teacher at Mooretown Public School, and then Benny Hill on his TV show who taught me, "When you assume, you make an ASS out of U and ME." People make misaligned choices like the ones above all the time because they assume. People can decide in this way for all sorts of reasons; perhaps they don't know who they really are, they're focusing on what life tells them matters, or they're making tradeoffs to gain the perks of their profession.

Barry told me he chose his role as the president of a logistics company instead of a more intellectually stimulating professional role, despite his high intellect, because he knew job security would never be an issue in this industry. He felt he had made a strategically-focused decision. He always led with his head and prided himself on making great choices, and for the most part he did. That is, if you leave mental stimulation or fulfilling personal relationships out of the equation.

Barry is carrying baggage packed tight with financial, relational, and health issues. He's older now. His choices have worked on one level – optics and lifestyle – and have not proved to be enough. He's empty, bored, and afraid of being alone.

It's not unusual to meet people at various stages and ages who check out mentally and do just what they have to do. Maybe they don't believe it can be different, maybe they don't know how to make it better, or, or, or ... If the strategy is developed to enable you to get through your life, then maybe this approach can work for you. Sometimes people excuse their non-involvement in work or life by adopting the notion of working to live rather than living to work. This is a poetic, idealistic mindset. I tried operating by it. I found that after working and sleeping and attending to my daily needs, there really wasn't much time left for living – until I realized that daily routine informs the quality of our existence. Blah!

Values are our greatest motivators. As I began to bring more of mine into everything I did, I began to enjoy the totality of my life with its daily potential and possibilities. It wasn't my idealism that was wrong; it was my approach: trying to honor me without making intentional changes. I wanted to make work something I enjoyed as an extension of me. Sales was a part of me, but the values of making relationships and making money were less important to me than self-satisfaction, meaning, and growth. Today I love working as a coach because it doesn't feel like my work but my vocation (which means "calling"). Coaching has allowed me to live a life on my terms and inspire and motivate people to find ways to live lives more on their terms for greater success.

The only wrong way to live is to take a lazy approach to your happiness and neglect understanding yourself to feel inspired. Who wants to just exist – to forgo enjoying every day?

Many left-handed people know how tough it is to be

forced to write with their right hand. Similarly, a big-picture person knows how hard it is to be in a role that requires them to account for every brushstroke. However, most people who make wrong choices and find themselves mismatched eventually stop noticing the stress they're creating for themselves. People are resilient. We can do anything we want, including putting up with lives that are harder than they need to be.

If this is true of you, this is a great time to be compassionate with yourself; nothing is written in stone and everything can be corrected. As in business, so in life: Conduct more due diligence, which always produces better results.

How clear are you on how you compromise your effectiveness? What if you knew your compromises meant you're not playing to win? Would you keep compromising?

Misalignment spins itself out in various challenges.

Think about what happens, for example, when task-oriented individuals are put in senior leadership roles that require skills to communicate their understanding of the company's strategy at the governance level; or when an introvert is given the role of painting the town with important visitors from foreign branches of the company. These types of traits are strategically important and yet are not considered in the overall selection process, and no one is better for it.

Perhaps you're forced as a leader to make do with an individual who has a natural sense of urgency but is in a slow, methodical process-oriented role. This is the greatest source of conflict and tension: the misalignment caused in our personal or professional relationships when those who need and want to take immediate action in an urgent way are dependent on others who are willing to wait longer than may be necessary for a great outcome to come to fruition. The costliest form of misalignment comes when a pleaser is given responsibility for results.

Unbeknownst to you, Mr. President, too many of your people have to plug in at home each night just to get through their job the next day. That's why your results are consistently compromised. That's why your margin for error is too great. That's why your results are only *good*.

People will always make these kinds of unconscious focus mistakes in their lives when they lack a compelling vision for more. For example, a big-picture thinker marries a detail person and neither gets to realize their natural orientation without a struggle – but hey, they're both cute. Or one person likes to operate at a blazing speed and the other likes to be more methodical and deliberate. How about IQ – what do you do with that? I didn't realize intellect was important to me and yet am not good with those who do not bring it forward. All approaches deliver results, but are they the results you want? Or are you okay always having to be among those people who change their pattern for the sake of the team? Nothing and no one wins when people are persuaded to act against their design and will. Not only do they stay the way they really are, but now they're resentful, too.

Regardless of how we come at life, there's always more than one way to skin that poor possum. It's natural for us to favor our approach, yet we are critical thinkers who can make adjustments when we recognize they're necessary. Using one of the examples above, it's easier for the person with a sense of urgency to be more deliberate than it is for the methodical thinker to pick up their responsiveness. Know how you want to realize results in life and throw out of the window the notion that opposites attract. We are meant to be who we are. Ask yourself if the approach you've allowed others to talk you into taking is enough for you. You may still decide an opposite of who you are is good for you; all options are possible and right as long as you're honoring your design and values and feel good for it.

Tradeoffs

Sometimes people focus on position and perks to sugarcoat the fact they're misaligned in their actual role. Professions, jobs, and partners are chosen often as a reaction to how others respond to them. When people go against their natural grain, they're more likely to become stuck in a life they don't really want. When we're looking for a mate or a work role, our challenge is to find how many of our must-have *values* are held in common. We often get caught-up in the emotions and dismiss our logic. Not a good strategy. We have been given emotions and logic. Both must always be used, to varying degrees.

Perhaps you chose this kind of tradeoff on purpose. If so, what did you have to give up? What's the impact of your tradeoff on you personally?

In the business and corporate environments where I work, it's easier to attribute strategy setbacks to a lack of buy-in caused by uninspiring compensation packages and unexpected market variables than it is to consider the misalignment of a leader who fails to inspire the troops to achieve greater results because he's in the wrong position, or because he's uninspired.

You may feel this is an impractical and oversimplified assessment of how misalignment can compromise results. Really? Take a look around you.

Achieving Alignment

A self-knowledge economy requires leaders to know their key people at an in-depth level. Leaders who ensure that their key people are firing on all cylinders create win/win solutions.

How much due diligence do you perform? Professionally and personally?

Don't get stuck with things how they are. Consider how they *could* be. The more your values are realized in all of the categories on the Wheel of Life, the more aligned you will be and the more success you will have.

Remember, the deepest alignment is when your *being*, who you are, shows up in your *doing*. The more you *be* who you are, and *do* as you are, the greater your alignment and the better your results.

We know what bores us to tears. We know what we tolerate to appease others. We know to whom, when, and where we willingly give our energy/power away. Stop tolerating what you do not "have to" tolerate. Have the courage to identify what you're tolerating.

We're also inspired by what inspires us. What if you were giving and receiving energy more than you were losing it? What would change in your life? What would you be saying yes to more often? What would you be saying no to more often?

Remember how ineffective compromise is. The suggestion that we're to find nobility in our ability to compromise is weak. What good is nobility when it's at the expense of self-respect and/or fulfilling results?

The alignment-informing profile tool I've been trained to use and employ as an expert focuses on high performance and alignment. It captures what it takes for each individual to be high-performing based on what's required in their role. Just as people have personalities, so do individual jobs.

I use this tool heavily in my professional and personal life, and will use it with my kids once they're young adults, at eighteen or so. The clearer we can be on who we are, the easier it is to know the values we have, and to make better choices regarding our careers and partners. That is, if we're serious about wanting different results. Knowing such things enables us to be our best and surround ourselves with the best so we can enjoy more of our lives.

For many years I wished I had more patience. I sometimes beat myself up for not having more of it. I wanted to be less intense because I knew my intensity was sometimes overwhelming for those around me. A lot changed in my life when I completed the profile myself and learned that my combination of intensity and results orientation makes me a change agent. I had wanted to be less intense so others would feel more comfortable and was trying to make myself less than I was. I stopped apologizing for wanting results *yesterday* and pursued only the companies and clients that could appreciate the value of such a trait and me.

This is part of my design and now I'm in choice to either mask it better, or assert it, to advance my objectives for my life. I've always been me, yet knowing this information and the implications allows me to finally walk taller and feel better about myself, and to win on my terms.

Life is stressful enough already. Why do we want to make it worse by compromising on results, wasting time or energy beating ourselves up, fighting, or denying who we really are?

WHAT ABOUT YOU?

- *Based on the description of alignment in this book, are you aligned in the key areas of your life to where your satisfaction comes from?*

- *What do you know you're just tolerating?*

- *What difference would more alignment in your life make?*

- *How might more alignment enable you to love yourself more?*

- *Where do you know you're wasting precious energy and time?*

- *How long will you accept this?*

- *Being unhappy and doing nothing is an indication you have resigned yourself to things. Do you want to live a life resigned to the way things are?*

Chapter 8

Personal Leadership

You can exert no influence if you are not susceptible to influence.

–Carl Jung

IN this part of the book we've been exploring the focus aspect of self-awareness and success. We've looked at values: clarifying which ones mean the most to us and discovering how we can align our choices, our identity, and our role with them. Now it's time to look at values and leadership.

I want to transcend the usual distinction between life and work, and the usual goal of bringing them into balance. I do so by seeing leadership as both a work and personal challenge. In our self-knowledge economy, personal and professional growth combine into what could be called personal leadership. As leaders in our families, communities, and work, our effectiveness and levels of satisfaction are an extension of our personal growth.

The key values that factor into the pursuit of leadership are **integrity**, **courage**, and **authenticity**.

Think about the kind of leadership that's possible from someone who has a slender sense of self. Shareholders should be concerned about the results such a CEO will generate. I certainly am when I meet one who is his or her own counsel, who isn't consistently inviting more objective, critical input from people outside the board. Such CEOs:

- Are growing stagnant in their role
- Are no longer considering the best interest of the organization
- Are not firing on all of their cylinders and aren't too concerned about it
- Do not want to be held more accountable, or
- Have not yet considered or found an effective accountability partner

What can be expected from a leader who lacks integrity to self by choosing not to focus more on self? The most effective leaders focus on alignment between their efforts and their feelings, values, choices, identity, role, and objectives.

Personal Growth

Bottom line, whether you're a corporate leader or on the front line, whether you're in the workforce or at home, personal growth isn't optional for you. Personal growth is what moves you from good to great. It's what makes you more successful than others. Many people already live by their values without being conscious of it. In fact, that's usually the case. The more conscious you can be of your values, however, and the more you seek to incorporate them, the more likely your efforts will lead to success. All of the roads of your life extend from who you are. That's why self-awareness and focus are mandatory for you; otherwise you'll sabotage yourself by allowing blind spots to form. Spend time getting to know yourself better. Understand your circumstances and connect to a purpose that means something to *you*.

How consistently do your choices (your actions) reflect your values? How aligned are they with what you know to be true about yourself?

After you take the time to work on yourself, you'll be ready to look at the key people around you and how they complement the master plan. What difference would it make to your results if you did this?

High Performance

Psychometricians have identified seven key traits that characterize high performance:

- Assertiveness
- Sociability
- Pace
- Detail Orientation
- Behavioral Adaptability
- Creativity
- Emotiveness

Eyeball your personal leadership in light of these traits and you just might learn some interesting things about yourself. Don't stop there, though, because your eyeballs are biased.

People are predictable; they're the ones who determine how effectively their or their leader's strategies are deployed.

That's why awareness-raising must start with you and extend to those around you.

In the spirit of efficiency, save yourself time, effort, and money by doing a different kind of due diligence up front. Not just the surface stuff to say something has been done to address matters. Make alignment a prerequisite of how you make your choices, whether they have to do with your partner, your career, people in your key roles, or how you live your life.

Stunted Leaders

I've worked with executives who don't really care about their company and/or product. Personal growth is out of the question. They do what their jobs need them to do. As a result, their intensity, conviction, and integrity in reaching objectives suffer. No one knows or really cares because everyone's busy and the results are good enough. There are always a myriad of reasons for these disconnects. It could be a misalignment issue. Maybe it got too tough for them to keep faking. Maybe there's a disconnect between their identity and what their job does or doesn't require. They may be meaning-seeking people who believe there's no meaning to be found in their work.

The enthusiasm and effectiveness of leaders waver when all they're pursuing are profits or meeting the needs of others. More often than not, these pursuits aren't inspiring or motivating enough for them. We all want to feel and know we're more than horses chasing the carrot. Don't let anything or anyone let you forget that for too long.

Unfortunately, most people do not actively seek to engage more of themselves. Engagement is generally not welcome. This is unfortunate because these same people are still expected to care. Yet how easy is it for them to care about something when they lack clear, direct, and naturally motivating reasons to care? People's drive, integrity, and focus usually begin to fade when their desire for more isn't nourished in their work or their life. Cutting this kind of corner – failing to address this reality – will contribute to the failure of any strategy. Leaders see greater results when they go beyond the bottom line and work with people to make sure they're in the right seat on the right bus.

This is the leadership road less traveled for a variety of reasons: It requires a lot of time; it's a soft cost that can't be justified; it may have a negative effect on the champions of an initiative if they think they're being doubted; it may reflect poorly on the strategy …

Think about how misalignment in leaders can stunt their leadership. For example, what's the impact of a leader who's responsible for results and when push comes to shove prefers to be liked? Or the impact of a leader who is most driven by methodology and "planfulness" and is in a role requiring active and ongoing understanding of changing variables in the market?

The recent Great Recession is an example of what happens when leaders are misaligned or strive for quick results without factoring in meaningful motivators or sound systems. That economic downturn was just as much about lazy, simplistic strategies as it was about having the wrong people in the wrong seats on the wrong bus. It's not enough to have everyone committed, verbally, to results. Strategies that are developed around the truth of the executioners – their motivators and drivers – will always be the most successful.

It's tough to find the right good people. It's much easier to develop strategies based on what and who you already have. If you don't like what you have and are only making do, then you're still kidding yourself and compromising on the results you might otherwise achieve, even if the roles in question were to remain vacant for a while.

Take my client Joe, a hugely successful millionaire.

He thinks big, he wants to change the world, and he has the drive, intellect, and heart to do so. Unfortunately, Joe is surrounded by people with an operational mindset – people who are always focused on a completely different end to the same opportunity.

In the self-knowledge economy, you're kidding yourself when you choose, for whatever reason, to overlook one of your strong personal values and think there won't be any related personal costs – for example, health. Have the courage to demand more of *you* in your strategies for life. Rust-out is just as prevalent as burnout, and sadder. We all need to feel fully engaged.

It's critical to the effectiveness of your strategy for you to know more than just the marketplace. You need to consider your key people's personalities and drivers. Your people's approach to achieving your objectives will affect your achievement of those objectives.

Leaders of Integrity

Have you ever considered the tangible costs of not putting sounder systems in place to support your executives, as people? What are the costs to you when these executives aren't really holding people accountable or are accepting too many excuses?

You know only what you know. Or to put it another way, you *don't* know what you *don't* know. What changes in the action plan could increase the likelihood of a more successful execution? What due diligence is missing from your strategy? Don't focus on the margin for error that's already in place; focus on holding yourself more accountable.

I've been a Dale Carnegie instructor and a Sandler Sales trainer. Training in such techniques can be hugely relevant for individuals in a company, as part of a broader strategy with a clear focus on expectations and measurements for the return on investment. These and the typical three-day courses in time management, balance, or stress can't be leveraged for maximum returns, however, unless adult learning styles are factored in. Expenditures on these programs are wasted when no accounting has been made for the need for ongoing reinforcement and retention of learning. Follow-up reinforcement is required to ensure the information is retained. This is how adults learn best, especially when they're beset with many competing claims on their interest and time.

Invest in Yourself

Regardless of how your journey to self-discovery plays out, don't limit yourself with self-doubt or because you believe you're not strong enough. All of us can tap into any of the values we want. We're hardwired to value certain things more than others. There's nothing you can't do; focus on what you want and develop a strategy to be successful. Make sure your strategy incorporates your ongoing need to learn more and do more for better results and to feel more alive. Of course we can't always do what we want to do. So consider what you *can* do so you can make better choices.

Have you considered the implications of following the status quo? Could you risk "failing forward," to go down fighting for something you believe in?

Invest in yourself to intentionally increase your knowledge of self. Be as clear as possible about what you want and the feelings you think you'll gain by attaining those pursuits. Ask yourself how important it is to you to feel that way. Don't judge your responses; there will be time for that. Keep the focus right now on what you can do from where you are to realize more success in your life. The process isn't as onerous as it may appear on paper. In fact, it's exciting and addictive.

WHAT ABOUT YOU?

- *How does your current personal leadership – your personal growth approach to business and life – satisfy your top ten values? Does it matter?*

- *Which values have you most honored in your life?*

- *Which values have you most missed in your life?*

- *What do you need to have more of in your life for your journey to be personally joyful?*

Chapter 9

A New Vision

Dream lofty dreams, and as you dream, so shall you become. Your vision is the promise of what you shall one day be; your ideal is the prophecy of what you shall at last unveil.

–James Allen

ALL this talk about focus leads us smack dab into the topic of vision. I prefer to call it a *new vision*, because part of the journey toward success is putting away our old vision of what our life *should be* – based on the expectations of our family, our society, and our workplace or profession – and seeing anew what our life *could be* when we align our choices and activities with the values that make us who we are.

Visions are personal and are experienced internally. They're a mental picture of something as if it already exists, even though the conditions necessary for it do not exist.

Visions are beautiful because they come from within us, which gives us cause to consider them and makes it easier to believe in them.

Knowing yourself enables you to trust your visions, because you know they're emanating from your key values.

Passion

It takes a lot to cast a vision and see it into being. It takes passion.

I've worked with more than one person and met tons of others who say they're not passionate about anything. They're not rejoicing in the fact; they're telling me because they're seeking more fulfillment and joy in their lives. They intuitively know passion is possible for them but have little sense of what they can feel passionate about.

Passion can of course be expressed harmfully. However, don't blame this powerful value of passion for how some people choose to manifest it. Passion in its intensity toward an emotion or experience fuels progress and inspiration. Electricity, airplanes, and computers may seem unrelated to passion, but these gains simply would not have been possible without it.

Passion isn't a sustainable emotion in and of itself; it requires effort. You either value it enough to make choices to bring it into your life or you don't. People's willingness to make that effort depends on their convictions and personality. Some so value what passion does for them, they're willing to deal with the uncertainty that may come with it. Others are willing to take some spin off their passion in favor of stability; they need only a little passion in their lives. Know what you want and need and choose your partner, and your job, accordingly. Bottom line: Passion provides the fuel for visions to become real to ourselves and others.

Vision and Change

Because visions are a portrait of what's possible, they're always about change. Visions are never about more of the same; they're about extending reality beyond what we already know. They're always about a better future. They're about seeing the invisible and making it visible. They're forward-focused.

People who have the courage to assert after what they believe in, even if only at first in their thoughts, are usually labeled and judged to be selfish. This is such a misguided notion. It's not selfish but courageous when people live by the values that are a part of their design. It's more selfish for others to deny them a chance to live with conviction, expecting them to maintain the status quo when that doesn't satisfy them. Expecting people to do what they don't believe in is asking them to sell out on themselves. Those who live without any conviction to standards of excellence judge those who are fueled by their passion.

Ask yourself how much thought you put into each day. Don't look at the number of things on your to-do list; look at how much of that list requires you to be present in body, mind, and soul. Take inventory of the choices you have made and where they have gotten you. Do they honor your fullness? What if you stopped listening to those people and institutions that want you to believe "It's not about you"?

What more could you bring to your life and to the world? It doesn't have to impress others; everything counts and makes a positive difference. Whether as a parent, professional, citizen, or as a person, be the change you want for your kids or for your life.

Progress – positive change – is always, at some level, the

outgrowth of dissatisfaction. Dissatisfaction is tremendously valuable because it helps us know there's more in us and for us we're not acting on. This kind of dissatisfaction promotes progress.

The world is divided by a "dissatisfaction line."

One side of the line is overcrowded. It's populated by those who are threatened by their own or others' feelings of dissatisfaction. They realize changing their reality will require more courage than they believe they have. So they focus on the good in their lives.

On the other side of the line are people who acknowledge their restlessness and pay attention to the possibility of change. They contribute their efforts and abilities to the cause of change. They accept their visions; they know and trust the path toward change will become clearer to them as they go.

As T.E. Lawrence put it, "All people dream, but not equally. Those who dream by night in the dusty recesses of their minds wake in the day to find that it was vanity; but the dreamers of the day are dangerous people for they may act their dream, with open eyes to make it possible."

WHAT ABOUT YOU?

- *What effort have you made to understand the visions you've had throughout your life?*

- *In what ways have your visions changed?*

- *In what ways did those changes reflect changes in you?*

- *How do you feel about those changes now?*

- *Which ones have you still not acted on? Why?*

Vision and Success

Visions aren't blind. They're not flaky. They're not pie in the sky for dreamers. They're based on a clear-eyed understanding of the possible. Visions are actualized by people who are open to possibilities and believe in something and believe in themselves.

Visions are about potential. Thoreau writes, "If one advances confidently in the direction of his dream, and endeavors to live the life which he has imagined, he will meet with a success unexpected in common hours."

What's the relationship between vision and success? They're synonymous. If you realize your vision, you're successful. Visions come from the soul and the soul is an extension of the Spirit. A vision is an act of focus and faith that is committed to always moving forward. You could say a vision is a realistic dream. When we dare to dream and note the possibilities, our vision will enlist our abilities to make it happen. Don't focus on all of the pieces of the vision that seem impossible; that may make the vision feel scary, edgy, or risky. Focus instead on having faith in what you feel is true for you.

Vision and Leadership

Meaningful change comes only when people are willing to take risks. That's why leadership and vision go hand-in-hand. All leaders out there, be they of a company, state, country, business, community, or family, are expected to be intentional about sharing their rich vision. There are leaders who lack vision and lack conviction, perhaps because the models they follow deny them passion. It's up to all of us to communicate our visions to the visionless so they can join us and achieve their own vision.

Jim, the president of a large company, is a good example

of vision and success. He committed himself to changing the culture of his organization from order-takers to proactive, relational salespeople. He did so by enlisting his must-have values in the battle to inspire his whole organization to excellence.

It wasn't easy for Jim. Not everyone shared his values. Those who did, excelled; those who didn't, remained stagnant. When he stated his vision he polarized his organization. His leadership team didn't share his idealism. They had no patience with the "soft values" he was always talking about. They wanted to stick to objective measurements such as budgeting and five-year plans.

"It's these people's *job* to help us reach our objectives," they told Jim. "Why do we need to talk about all this airy-fairy vision stuff?"

The company's workers, however, did sign on to Jim's vision. It was precisely the soft values that inspired them to earn hard money for the firm and themselves. Jim understood that, though we work for money to live, we are three-dimensional people. We are more engaged when our mind and soul are in concert with what the body needs.

It took a while – till after the next very positive quarterly report, to be honest – but Jim's leadership team eventually caught the vision, too, because he had the conviction and passion to keep painting the picture for them.

Yes, business success is a function of market variables, competitive advantage, strategic objectives, data crunching, emerging markets, trends, margins, and returns. Those factors are necessary and important. However, any strategy that does not also factor softcore information into this mix is doomed to failure. For example, the lack of soft information creates strategic ineptitude in *planning/forecasting* and *defining objectives*. Maximum success is not reached because of the failure to incorporate all relevant realities. When we do this, we operate in the short term and get good results.

Be careful here. You don't want to be known for sustaining competitive *dis*advantage.

The new vision demands we seek greatness from and for ourselves and then for and from others. Our best will then inspire and influence others to do the same. I'm not calling for a group hug or to bring donuts in for everyone. I'm trying to inspire you to reach the Valley – a metaphorical place for those who seek a purposeful existence and want to focus on contribution that reading Ayn Rand introduced me to, a place I've longed for ever since.

When Visions Are Most Powerful

Visions are relevant and worth understanding. They're the soul's way of indicating possibility. In and of themselves, though, they remain just another thought among the countless ones we have each day. They have the potential to release great power when we realize our soul is communicating directly to us. Our soul knows things we don't know and gives us visions that seem impossible. I never thought someone like me could have a show and then enough content to even fill a book. When we trust and have faith, anything is possible. That's why I remain open to my visions and lead with possibilities.

Understandably, we don't always want to listen to our soul. To trust something so intangible seems flaky. I've finally decided to give in to my soul, though, because it knows and I don't want to keep wasting time. Absent other options, what else can we do when the status quo is no longer an option?

Unfortunately, people don't realize that vision is enough. Vision will provide us with the steps to take, using our values, personality, and mindset. Don't you get it? Our values come from the same source that communicates our visions to us. Do the math: We are set up to be successful!

It may seem crazy to think it's possible to exist and thrive by honoring our values and following our visions. Society and church tell us not to. Society gives us the framework for how we're to live. Church tells us we are destined to keep failing and will never reach perfection and then assigns nobility to our puny efforts in that direction. Society and church may have their own reasons for not wanting us to grasp that we've been designed to succeed, that we can do anything, that we don't have to struggle, and that life doesn't have to be hard. In fact, the opposite is the case. The more you know about yourself, the less you struggle and the more time you have to be successful. The struggle associated with changing the world, or developing new products, or making changes in our life is not a struggle when we listen to our visions and apply our values with passion.

While it's okay not to know the steps to take, it's never okay to let go of the vision. You'll be haunted if you do. Letting go of vision is the genesis of regret.

WHAT ABOUT YOU?

- *What are the recurring thoughts and desires of your heart?*

- *What have some of your visions been?*

- *For what reasons did you let a vision go?*

- *Have you ever focused on a new vision?*

- *What new visions could you focus on now?*

Part 3

Strategy

$$\begin{array}{r} \textit{Self-Awareness} \\ + \qquad \textit{Focus} \\ + \qquad \textbf{\textit{Strategy}} \\ \hline = \textbf{\textit{SUCCESS}} \end{array}$$

Chapter 10

Free at Last!

If we all worked on the assumption that what is accepted as true were really true, there would be little hope of advance.

–Orville Wright

A quick recap:

• *Self-awareness* is the most powerful tool at our disposal to produce change. By developing our awareness, we make better choices that bring us more success. Being self-aware translates into honoring our needs: body, mind, and soul.

• *Focusing* on and aligning what matters to us – our feelings, values, choices, identity, and role – and then using that focus, steeped in self-awareness, empowers us to create better professional and personal results. When we get clear on our measurements for success and then get our ladder against the right wall, we have more success. When we're focused on what we know matters to us, we're more likely to get where we're going.

Now we come to the strategy part of my formula. Strategy is the pivot point between self-awareness and focus, on the one hand, and results (success), on the other. Looked at from the shadow of our visions, strategy is the process that gets us to success. This process involves making choices that are aligned with our values and that achieve excellent results. All of the meaningful data converge in the strategy into an action plan for success.

My Favorite Clients

I'd like to introduce you to the type of client I particularly enjoy working with in my practice. You may fit their profile already or may be at an earlier stage in your journey.

These clients are usually fifty-five plus. They have worked their way through life based on their early training, focusing on their dependents and their job first and their own life and values second. Perhaps it's the imminence of their retirement years that is motivating and enabling them to take a hard look at their own lives and consider a new standard of excellence.

They're learning to acknowledge some of the choices they've made. They're open to looking at how those choices have served them. Most of them don't come to me focused on the particulars of their job; they come wanting to focus on themselves in all of their roles. They're no longer willing to be all about their job. They want a new vision.

Most of my clients are married, have kids, and have good

lives. They're willing now to listen to their intuition and focus on more than just work and all of their responsibilities. They wonder what a life that is not ninety percent directed toward work could look like. They know they can't keep living the way they've lived. They're nervous about having to hang out with the spouse they have little in common with. They think about consulting but they're not so sure they want to spend more of their lives and time on the same old repetitive business cycles and challenges. They're asking how much time they want to spend with the grandkids or pursuing that elusive perfect game of golf.

Simply put, these clients are in action mode. They're focused on developing strategies to realize broader results, strategies that factor in their personal value, including their desire for more zest in their daily existence. They're able to consider not just one or two aspects of their life but the whole shootin' match and develop better strategies for it.

It's as if they're saying to destiny, "Okay, I played it your way all this time and it only marginally got me what I really wanted. Now let's try it a bit my way. What if ...?"

Consider the case of Sally and Todd.

Sally, for the sake of family stability and for the optics of being the mother of a perfect family, has been willing to overlook Todd's infidelities with women at the office and elsewhere throughout his long career as the president of a successful firm. She uses her strong personality to push Todd into a tradeoff: He's allowed his infidelity to their marriage as long as he's faithful to the children and the family unit.

How could anyone find integrity when living based on that kind of model? Sally denies Todd positive feelings of self-worth. He wants to leave but allows guilt to immobilize him and acts weak. No one wins, least of all the kids, who are now nicely launched into their own dysfunctional relationships.

When Todd came to see me, it was out of intuitive curiosity; he knew it would help him be a better businessman.

He wasn't interested in having to change much; he just wanted third-party objectivity about his future. Everything was all right in his business, but he knew his private life was having a negative effect on his role and his company.

As we worked together, Todd identified with such values as tradition and duty, though he did not revere them – they were not among his must-haves for a joyous life. Tradition and duty were strong values in his family environment as he grew up. Todd approached his life, he said, with logic, practicality, and intellect because he knew the kids would benefit from sound systems. He was living a double life, though: He knew the models he was teaching them were what got him where he was personally. He knew they didn't work.

When we explored his values, he changed. That's the only way to describe it. Courage and conviction had been absent from most of his life. When he finally decided to build on those values, he was a better person for it. He shifted his focus to himself, to his own personal satisfaction, to the passion available for everyone once he stopped playing the charade his life had become.

You can imagine how much a monkey like this weighs on leaders' shoulders, how much it keeps them from operating at their best.

The clients I've been describing find it difficult to profess to wanting more outside their jobs. They already have pretty much everything. They know "Oh right, poor you" would be the response if they expressed their needs to anyone. They struggle with how they can explore their real desire to finally look inside themselves when they had thought for so many years the objects of their desire were in the driveway, the boardroom, or the bedroom.

People are being more entrepreneurial these days. They're not so ready to hop on – or stay on – a corporate bandwagon, despite the steady paycheck and benefits. More women are daring to stand on their own two feet. They, and many men, too, are making choices for self over other tradition-ally competing demands and expectations. Whole societies in oppressive countries are standing up and demanding freedom.

People seem to be listening more to their Spirit and wondering what else is possible for them in their lives.

The specific opportunities my clients bring to the table are forward-focused. We leverage their existing realities into strategies that will net them more success, both profession-ally and personally.

They're ready to exit the blame game. While they acknowledge they may not have been taught to focus on self and strategize through visions, they admit they hadn't expended much energy looking beyond what was right in front of them.

Focus on Self-Awareness

The very first strategy step is to make sure you have holistic awareness, starting with yourself, and then to sharpen your focus accordingly. Go back to what you've read regarding self-awareness and focus and build on those concepts. Pay special attention to your must-have values and check out how aligned they are with your choices, identity, and role.

This process takes great strength and vigilance. It won't be easy to resist the gravitational pull of your critics.

Your Inner Critic

For example, if you have started on this journey, you may have already been confronted, challenged, and stopped by your inner critic. This is a self-appointed judge who jumps on you for any idea outside the norm. Your inner critic tries to keep you focused on your instinct for security and society's demand for the status quo.

Expect resistance from within. Be prepared for it. Don't

give in to it. I encourage my clients to give their inner critic a name, so they can push back directly whenever it counsels them to abandon their strategy.

Your Outer Critics

You can also expect outer critics to heave into view. They may be members of your extended family or your own family; they may even be colleagues at work or friends – bottom line, there will be no shortage of them.

Too many people are ready to make us feel unrealistic for considering more than good. So few of them aspire for great, and they certainly don't want you to remind them how safe they're playing. Yet it's part of our DNA to seek growth, progress, and evolution. It doesn't matter whether we're the Queen of England or John Doe: It's quite natural to want more.

When we do choose to focus on self, we just have to look more closely at our world to see trends that are clear extensions of what self-awareness enables: unlimited possibilities in a changing world.

While history is paved with examples of those who have done great things and amassed much wealth or other benefits for themselves and others, we generally view them as special people who were smarter and luckier and had more going for them to begin with. This attitude is changing, however. Today more people are open to trusting that they do know through their intuitions and that with this knowledge they can choose to focus on their strategy.

It's actually becoming fashionable to use personal criteria in determining direction, plans, and focus. More and more people want to feel alive and have it all.

Work from the Inside Out

Ask yourself: How much difference could more personal information, about me and others, make to my strategies for achieving results? Explore this question and act on the answers you get. You'll gain a definite strategic advantage.

When will you challenge more of your comfort zones, not in unethical, disrespectful ways, but to look more broadly?

Remember, living life on your terms means working from the inside out. Start with who you are. As will be discussed in more detail in the next and final part of this book, your definition of success comes from how *you* desire it, how *you* define it, how *you* pursue it.

We always need a strategy to get to where we're going. My strategy is to trust my visions and intuition and work from there.

What will your strategy be? Have you ever defined what personal greatness could be for you?

Taking the time to be clear on what greatness could look like in our lives takes us off autopilot. It disperses our complacency. It inspires us to encourage others to keep striving. It prompts us to keep asking one another questions about what's next. (We no longer fear being asked these questions ourselves.) Instead of persuading ourselves to be content with the goodness we've already achieved, and instead of claiming nobility for giving up what we really want, we stay true to our visions and take action to achieve them.

Once you have your objective, your strategy will extend from where you have focused your self-awareness, and you'll have more success.

My clients aren't always comfortable with the idea of having to factor self into their strategies. This approach seems odd to them. They believe business is about business and the self stuff is a whole different journey. Many are used to leaving who they are in the trunk of their car when they get to work – and bringing out yet another self when they go home again.

When your desire is personal fulfillment, anything is possible. This is the one pursuit in life, the one journey, where the measurements for success come only from within. You're in control.

Spend some time with your own strategy for success. Make sure it's yours, and that it's meaningful, motivating, and inspiring. Being able to do this is a good indicator that you're looking at life from the inside out.

WHAT ABOUT YOU?

- *At what point in the strategy development of your business or life did you factor in other people's effectiveness?*

- *How do you use this information for better results?*

- *How do you handle the inconsistencies in your life?*

Chapter 11

Strategies Are About the How

What do you want to achieve or avoid? The answers to this question are objectives. How will you go about achieving your desired results? The answer to this you can call strategy.

–William E. Rothschild

WE all use strategies and benefit from having them, regardless of the outcomes we're seeking. We employ strategies as ways to realize objectives, be they for the house, family, or business. Strategies are action plans designed to achieve specific goals.

In the previous chapter, we dealt in an introductory way with the importance of strategy in the process of realizing success from stronger self-awareness and focus. Now, in this chapter, let's look at the "how" of strategy.

Planning

As obvious as it may sound, strategies require planning. Strategy is about preparing; it's about being able to receive, respond, and advance as more focus is brought to both present and emerging opportunities, trends, and markets.

If you've taken the time to focus on what's coming for you personally or professionally, ask yourself: How prepared and able am I to leverage and actualize these opportunities?

The more strategically we plan, the better poised we are to action better strategies for better ROI. The world is unfolding as it should. Trust that and keep planning and paying attention to the right end of the opportunity.

Unsound Strategies

There are a ton of strategies out there to follow: approaches that have worked for other successful CEOs and companies. It's natural for us to think all we have to do is adopt a model we like and follow it to get the same results as someone else who succeeded with it. Many of us take this approach with our bodies. For example, we may want a perfect "ripped" body. Trouble is, we think hardcore exercise will get us there even though we continue eating a diet of empty calories. Think of how many times you've adopted only parts of an effective strategy and still felt entitled to all of the same results. When that occurs, do you then blame the strategy or model for not getting you there?

To achieve specific progress, deeper thought is required. We can gently let our mind direct us, and do course checks along the way, to ensure that we're learning what we most need to know. That also requires us to look more closely for the inconsistencies between our strategies and our objectives. The better you can understand the values behind the vision of the strategies you're advancing, the better your personal buy-in.

Larry is a good example of this. Because his strategy is not based on the totality of his values, he must pump himself up and don his Teflon suit just to enter the office door each day. The misalignment between his role and his values causes him to act out: He's adding to his stress at work by encouraging his wife to quit her job to raise child after child. He's limiting his choices. What could be more stressful than that?

In his Faustian bargain for the perks of his job, Larry has promised to dedicate his life to his multinational company as its CEO. His company owns him. It has put him on a short leash. He's lucky to get out for a walk once in a while.

Larry admitted to me his life isn't so enjoyable. He is stressed to the max. We focused on the behaviors he must sustain to keep his charade going. He fears he will lose too much if he gets off the corporate roller-coaster. We then focused on his deepest values, which turned out to be **family, self-respect**, and **love**. His personality traits were along the same line; they focused on being accommodating – not exactly a trait required to be a high-performing CEO. He was seriously misaligned in his body, mind, and soul. At the same time, he didn't like the types of roles his personality *was* best suited for. He rejected his design in favor of his ego.

As Archie Bunker would put it, Larry painted himself into a corner and threw away the keys. His personal choices require him to stay in a job because he has promised his wife the optics that are important to her and therefore needs the money to fund those choices.

Larry has played this game his whole life. He learned early what people are drawn to and has played to that. Nothing in his job comes naturally to him, because his role and tasks do not flow from his personality traits. He doesn't like to hold people accountable; he's quite willing to accept excuses, and overlooks ineffectiveness for longer than is good for the company. His company therefore does not have a CEO with the traits required to do the job with excellence. Larry is good. He's really good. However, it comes at a huge cost to him because none of it comes naturally. He's really a process and operations guy, not a big-picture strategist or risk-taker. So he puts in the extra hours, making sure all the *t*'s are crossed and *i*'s dotted – and that everyone is wowed by his performance.

No matter how much Larry fakes it, he'll never be the kind of leader he pretends to be. His first instinct is in a direction opposite from what's needed. In times of stress, Larry will always revert to who he really is. It takes a lot of work for him to keep this up. Some on the board are beginning to question Larry's approach. At the same time, the board loves the good results he brings and how dedicated he is to the company. Now he's being transferred to head up a different division of the company overseas.

This CEO is slowly killing himself. While his external validators are satisfied, he has checked out of his life emotionally. He has surrendered his life to the world's flawed external models. Everyone loses, except the wife, who never wanted to have to work anyway.

Just this morning I met with Oliver, who told me his fulfillment doesn't matter as long as the family is good. (And he meant it – gag!) People just don't want to see that their strategies end up limiting everyone, including themselves, *and the family's not good.*

Mike enjoys a moderate life. He eats well, exercises, and enjoys his wine. However, he's imploding. Various parts of his body are causing him huge problems. He accepts his role as the sacrificial lamb for the sake of the cause. He's bored with his life and ready for new things, but he's tolerating the disconnect between his values and his life. Mike has accepted this tradeoff for himself. His body hasn't. It's turning on him, asking him to address the needs of his soul. Mike is slowly getting there. We have worked together for more than three years. He seems to be leaning a lot on his value of creativity to help him develop.

Do any of these examples describe you? Are you aware that doing nothing about it means your corpse will be among the many others who knew neither victory nor defeat? It doesn't have to be that way. You can avoid this fate through mental effort and self-understanding. You have all it takes to do it. Besides, aren't you ready to stop wimping out on yourself? Isn't it time for you to put better strategies in place?

Sound Strategies

The more we ask ourselves before, during, and after the execution of our strategy whether we truly believe what we believe, the more room we give our strategies to be effective.

Remember, the strategies that enabled you or your company to succeed at one point in your evolution are unlikely to keep working as time goes on. A different lens must be used to understand new possibilities and challenges as you cross the chasm to a different level of effectiveness. It's the same for individuals. Being in growth mode includes developing the right strategies to cross the chasm. That's just the way life is. You get to choose whether you'll struggle and always be reactive in your strategy development or will equip yourself and win on your terms.

Sound business strategy requires a deep knowledge of your company's strengths, capabilities, and objectives combined with a realistic view of your competition and changes in the industry and market. Sound personal strategy requires an objective awareness of yourself and all those who will influence your results directly. It also requires a clear focus on what you wish to achieve. The strategies that account for the relevant variables – including personality traits, strengths, blind spots, and levels of commitment – deliver better results.

The Five Fundamentals of Strategy

Since strategies are about how we plan to achieve our objectives, it's useful to consider Sun Tzu's five fundamentals of strategy as laid out in his famous *The Art of War* (sixth century BC). In the following fourteen statements he deals with the five fundamentals of strategy: Mission, Change, Ground, Leadership, and Art.

1 The Art of Strategy is of vital importance to the nation.

2 In situations of life or death, it is the way of winning or defeat; its study cannot be ignored.

3 Therefore, before any confrontation, analyze the five fundamental elements of strategy and compare the results for all involved.

4 The first is Mission: The second is Change. The third is Ground. The fourth is Leadership. The fifth is Art.

5 The Mission inspires people to be in complete unity with their leaders. Therefore, they will join in regardless of any danger even for their lives.

6 Change is yin and yang, right or wrong, and the systems of time.

7 The Ground is where the confrontation takes place; it is obstructed or easy, far or close, the chances of winning or defeat.

8 Leadership is ability, credibility, humaneness, bravery, and discipline.

9 The Art is a flexible system of skills brought to the ground of operation.

10 Leaders must be familiar with these five; those who know them well will win and those who don't will be defeated.

11 When analyzing the five fundamentals, examine each one carefully for all involved in the confrontation.

12 Now tell me: Which side has a Mission? Which Leader has ability? Which Leader can influence Change and the Ground? Which side has Art? Which strategy has strength in numbers? Which side is highly trained? Which side has fair rewards and penalties?

13 It is through these calculations that I sense triumph or defeat.

14 If leaders who listen to my calculations are employed, they are certain to win; retain them. If leaders who do not listen to my calculations are employed, they are certain to be defeated; remove them.

In the context of this book and my formula, *Mission* is about conviction to the cause and integrity to the vision you want your strategy to address. This is about self-awareness and focus. You could substitute the word "vision" for "mission," in the sense that great leaders who cast a vision inspire people to go on a mission to create the conditions that will make the vision come true. This reality is what's behind Sun Tzu's emphasis on the complete unity of the people, in concert with their leaders – alignment.

To factor in the role of *Change*, actively incorporate the

Laws of the Universe. (See chapter 13.) A great challenge comes into play here: simultaneously focusing on your values and vision while allowing for and accepting the contradictions of the yin/yang of life. The more information you have, the more likely you are to realize success.

The *Ground* involves the realities you're up against at the point of execution. Great leaders look through the lens of Mission and the realities of Change to get an accurate view of the battlefield.

Then it's a matter of applying *Leadership* and *Art* to make optimal use of realities on the ground.

Leadership, whether you have a title placing you in a leadership role or not, is about wisdom, integrity, compassion, courage, and severity. Or to put it another way, intensity and conviction to the cause.

Art is in how we operate our lives: how organized our minds are, how clear we are on who we are and what we're capable of, and how we exercise responsibility in the management of our resources, both soft and hard, and both personal and organizational.

Mind Your Own Focus

It's a strategic error in any game – from Scrabble and Chess to an advertising campaign or war in a far country – to become focused on the opponent's strategy. That's what we do when we're not confident in our own strategy. We're unsure; we're wavering; we're reactive; we're ready to settle too quickly. We can't create effective strategies when we're not clear in our own focus. Worse, we're in danger of actually adopting our opponent's strategy and forgetting all about our own. Guess who wins then?

Optimal Mindsets and Behaviors

Strategies and the techniques for implementing them are most powerful when they come from a compelling mindset. It's stressful for a person to be open-minded and flexible in their strategy when their mindset is primarily based on what has been tried, tested, and proven. In contrast, people who operate from a mindset focused on possibilities will be attracted to new ways to reach better results. Their self-awareness gives them the courage and confidence to set parameters on how far and how long the experimentation goes. Such people operate from an optimal mindset.

As for optimal behaviors, these include a willingness to test hypotheses, challenge processes, and even consider other hypotheses about possibilities.

It's tempting to take up residence in the land of possibility, and it's more exciting to get into action! What's holding you back? What can you do to minimize that limitation?

Faith creates optimal behaviors. As one of your top ten values, faith will enable more than you're likely or even able to do on your own. Faith makes the difficult easier. Faith doesn't replace effort; it shows you the beauty, magic, hope, and inspiration available to you to get you through the dark days, the days when you don't know anything more than your vision.

I'm not talking about blind faith or lazy faith. Faith requires action on all levels: body, mind and soul. Personally, you'll get into action mode and start to see different results in your life when you deepen your awareness of your own values and use focus and strategy to align your *doing* with your *being*. Professionally, it's the same. The results will flow, guaranteed.

I realize today's dynamic markets and technologies have called into question the possibility of sustaining competitive advantage. There's always pressure in organizations to improve something – for example, productivity, quality, or speed. Leaders embrace such tools as Total Quality Management, benchmarking, and reengineering to realize operational improvements. I refer to these management techniques to highlight how these competitive advances are really great only when the right conditions exist. While this is less arbitrary than the positioning of the sun and moon, it is not useful and relevant for everyone. Even when these techniques *are* applicable, they're rarely translated into truly consistent, sustainable profitability.

My strategy is very simple. It works in all types of companies and situations. Its only wild card is the self-awareness piece of the formula, which informs the outcome. However, people are predictable. Personal and professional evolution and growth are the byproduct of strategies and focus that account for this deeper awareness. No matter how you slice it and in what culture you place it, this formula may be tapped strategically and with integrity. Doing so will net organizations and individuals more success than if they keep doing more of the same or run after the latest management fad.

Realizing success isn't rocket science. Success is the natural reward of following a formula or process that works. More success is realized when greater personal satisfaction matters, too. There's so much more inside you to tap for your greater gain. It's up to *you* to get serious about wanting better results for yourself and developing strategies to get there.

WHAT ABOUT YOU?

• *What are your personal strategies for success?*

• *Who is in control – you or someone/something else?*

• *Where do you focus your strategies?*

• *Did you know it's possible to limit surprises if you accept that people are predictable?*

• *How can you use that information to benefit your strategy?*

• *Where do you think you would have realized different results if you had factored more self-awareness into your decisions?*

Chapter 12

Creative Tension

Creative tension comes from seeing clearly where we want to be, our vision, and telling the truth about where we are, our current reality. The gap between the two generates a natural tension.

–Peter Senge

IT'S interesting to consider the different ways people react to the gaps between where they are and where they want to be.

The more passive lessen the tension by ignoring the gap and making do with what they already have.

Others act out against the tension by spinning off into dysfunctional behavior.

They use people, drugs, sex, or workaholism to mask the reality of what they lack.

And then there are those who look at their life, acknowledge the disconnect between where they are and what they want for themselves, and are willing to live in the gap while they close it in their favor.

Creative tension is invaluable. It can provide the fuel and energy that conviction requires. If succeeding was effortless, everyone would be successful.

In moments of creative tension, remind yourself of the best possible outcome of your effort. Creative tension requires more of *you*. It requires you to put aside the props of wishing on a star or just repeating a mantra; on their own, these do nothing to address the creative tension you're feeling. If you choose "letting go" as your strategy, that will only lower your expectations and affirm your desire to reduce the uncomfortable tension. Focusing on unrealistic strategies could just invite more frustration. When you're clear on the best of you, it's easier for you to know how to close the gap in your favor. Your strategy will be strengthened for better personal results.

I can't promise you immediate changes, nor can I tell you how your courage will be rewarded. I *can* say learning to live in this kind of tension will make you stronger. Being okay with not knowing how things will play out will increase your ability to see and deal creatively with your possibilities on a day-to-day basis. This is true for big-picture thinkers and people whose days are dominated by details.

You must still be you. Focus a bit on that part of you. Get clear on which details will most help reduce your creative tension and focus on addressing those. Creative tension is a reality for anyone who has aspirations to truly live. It's the price of entry for success. As Miley Cyrus sings in her song "The Climb":

The chances I'm taking
Sometimes might knock me down
But no, I'm not breaking.

I'm mostly okay with this kind of tension because my approach to life values **intensity**, **urgency**, and **results**. My challenge is to slow my mind down, step back, and not get too frustrated. In integrity to this new path I've chosen for myself, I accept that delays are par for the course. I'm not good at dealing with them, and accept that they too shall pass. My formula of **Self-Awareness + Focus + Strategy = Success** reminds me that slowing down does not necessarily compromise intensity; it just focuses it better and I benefit. I combine my formula with regularly scheduled meetings with an objective third party, my coach. Our objective is to focus my efforts for maximum results. This usually results in more clarity for forward-focused movement and better results.

Trust vs. Control

Living with creative tension is supported by learning to *trust* more than *control*. This is a challenging choice to honor. It certainly is for me. As mentioned earlier, it's much easier for me to exert control because whether my efforts work or not, at least I feel I'm taking charge of my life.

I'm learning that taking a trusting approach makes it easier for me to live by my values. Acting on my intuitions means I'm less likely to take action for action's sake. My actions are increasingly an extension of my values, which are what motivate me.

The world is complicated and people all have agendas. I'm not deft or smart enough to know how to get to where my visions seem to be leading me. It seems that is how it goes with visions: They keep speaking to us regardless of our inability to understand everything about them and their implications. Is that to mean, or suggest, that the Source from which they come will enable us to realize them?

It's not easy for me, as a Type A personality, to trust, yet I value efficiency, and the strategy of trusting is working better for me than when the direction of my life was only up to me. Sure, control will get me somewhere, but I want to follow the most efficient and effective direction so I can sit back in fulfillment and enjoy more of the fruits of my labor. Trusting enables me and helps me put stress and setbacks into perspective. It is hard, but it always works.

The only right choice is to actively participate in your own life's journey in the first place by actively engaging in all of it with your body, mind, and soul. From there, your responses to the opportunities that come your way will add up to the choices that most define your life.

I realize this isn't a very concrete strategy and therefore may not feel very useful to you. It seems easier when someone tells us what to do. At least then we can blame them. Except it's your life and only you know what you want.

What would happen if you incorporated more trust into your strategy development? Try it. Start small and let me know how it goes. How could trusting yourself not work?

Think of it this way: When you invite people to your house, you show them how to accomplish their objectives while they're there. Maybe you show them where the bathroom is, where they'll be sitting during dinner, where you keep the scotch or the TV. You point the kids to the playroom. The guests trust you to help them maximize their time in your home.

In the same way, we are guests in this world. We've been invited in and given objectives to reach while we're here. Control dictates that we do whatever we need to do to reach our objectives. Trust dictates that our strategy will flow from our self-awarenesses and focus.

You can lift the stress of having to always live the right

way by trusting you'll be shown what you need when you need it. This isn't to encourage you to do nothing; it's to remind you to stay broad in your strategy development and be clear on what you're developing your strategy to reach.

Intuition, Risk, and Living

One of the ways to move from controlling to trusting is to move from thinking to intuiting. When we think a problem through, we're analyzing and calculating. We're in control. When we delay that very appropriate response of analyzing and calculating till after we have considered, in stillness, our intuitions, we will receive our mind's immediate understanding of something we can't yet explain. It's then that we can best use our abilities.

Relying on our intuitions more than our thoughts – trusting the knowledge that comes from our soul – can feel risky. Yet we have been created with the ability to know in this way. And how risky is it, really, to trust what we're feeling? Remember, the risk we're taking is on ourselves. We may not like that idea. But there's no risk more worth taking than on yourself. That is not really risking: It's living. The question, therefore, isn't about how willing we are to take a risk but how willing we are to live.

Intuition vs. Instinct

Intuitions are different from instincts. Each has a different function to play, and they don't always work in concert. Instincts are mostly learned, and are historical in their rationale. They're always a function of the devil we know. We know how things always work and via our brain waves we know what our responses had better be.

Our instincts don't evolve; they're static and in place to protect us, telling us whether to fight or flee. Our instincts seek to minimize the threats. Our intuitions are very spiritual and accurate, because they come from within and are situational. They guide us on a case-by-case basis.

We don't need to rely on our instincts as the gatekeeper of our lives. We're no longer in danger of being eaten by wolves or killed by the next cave dweller over. It's time for us to engage our intuitions.

Try doing that right now. Put the book down and consider what you have read. Do you feel prompted in any way? Perhaps to reject the simplicity of the contents of this book and stay committed to your old vision? Or are you being nudged by your intuition to read on?

The distinction between intuition and instinct is critically important because of its implications for the way we live and how we treat others.

Allow me to introduce you to Richard, a strong, successful, wealthy jerk. He knows how the system works and plays it to his advantage. He has the looks and other trappings most women want. His focus is on making money and making sure his needs are met. He considers the bigger, broader world only insofar as it affects his world.

One of Richard's colleagues told him he should consider working with my firm. My contracts are usually nine months in duration. I canceled the contract with Richard after two months. I liked Richard – he could be charming – but he was mostly faking it. He was unkind to those outside of his sphere of influence. The way he flirted with women masked a fundamental disrespect.

Richard trusted only his instincts and his intellect. Together the two enabled him to be very powerful and effective in his numbers-focused role as a managing director. He liked to control; trusting wasn't tangible enough for him. His resistance to his intuitions exposed the limitedness of his mindset.

We're all allowed to be and feel how we choose; ideally

we minimize the intentional damage we cause others and the world and show fairness to all. When our reliance is mostly on our instincts, however, we will tend to live out of a mentality of scarcity, focused on meeting our needs – and to hell with others. (Jean-Paul Sartre's apt expression is, "Hell is other people.")

Now let me introduce you to George, a man who is strongly intellectual and intuitive. This is a very challenging potential values clash, and yet George usually gets these two strengths and values working together.

George came to see me because he was at an impasse. He was intuitively aware that he wasn't bringing more of his most important values into his life. As a successful partner in an advertising agency, he was comfortable and satisfied – and not happy. Fortunately, he decided to take the risk of increasing his self-awareness. Bringing his intellect and intuition into a creative partnership, he focused more on who he knew himself to be.

George wasn't looking to change the world around him; he cared about how he was feeling on the inside, because he wanted his mojo back.

WHAT ABOUT YOU?

- *What most informs the day-to-day use of your intellect, intuition, and instincts?*

- *How is this working for you?*

- *What's still missing?*

- *What are you allowing to deny the feelings you wish to have?*

- *What's your strategy to address the void this creates?*

Chapter 13

Laws of the Universe

There is orderliness in the universe, there is an unalterable law governing everything and every being that exists or lives. It is not a blind law, for no blind law can govern the conduct of living beings.

–Mohandas Gandhi

LET'S close this part of the book, on strategy, by looking at some amazing strategy tools: the laws of the universe. These laws have been put into words and a system of collective wisdom by New Thought and New Age leaders and writers in this and the past century. They're a blend of Western and Eastern religion and philosophy. As I've seen in my life and my practice, success in the self-knowledge economy I've been talking about throughout this book comes from absorbing and acting on sources of knowledge that have been proven to be effective. We need high-quality information, information that is timeless and therefore absolute. That's what these laws provide. They're especially powerful when the seeker already has personal knowledge to build from.

Study these laws. Explore them. Incorporate them and your greater self-understanding into your strategies and approach, to realize greater success. These laws, if you take the time to understand them, represent high-level information that you can convert into active knowledge to achieve consistent higher-quality results. Remember, a new effort is always required to achieve different results. Use these laws as the cherry on the top of your strategy, not as your only strategy.

Yes, I've worked with many people, and know of many others, who have realized greater success without consciously incorporating these laws or other prescriptions into their strategies. Thankfully, there's more than one path to any destination. However, using the contents of this book, including these laws, will help you find your path and realize more personal satisfaction.

The premise of these laws is that we live in a universe that works by predictable, repeatable, and understandable laws. This is true of both the tangible and intangible realities in which we live. We're subject to physical laws such as the law of gravitation. We're also subject to laws that transcend the physical and govern the spiritual realm, though they're not formally sanctioned or acknowledged by organized religion.

The laws of the universe address the body/mind/soul complexity of humans. Knowing them helps us navigate between the different planes on which we live. The better we understand how to live effectively within all three planes of our existence – body, mind, and soul – the more fulfillment, peace of mind, and joy we will have.

These laws establish the intelligent makeup and processes of this world. They level the playing fields of life. Anyone who understands and employs them has a chance to make it. Consider how the laws could work for you so you can realize a more natural, flowing life. Life was not meant to be a struggle; it was meant to be a daring, exciting adventure.

What follows isn't a complete summary and explanation of all of the laws; it's just a teaser to interest you in learning more about them to realize greater gains.

The Law of Perpetual Transmutation/ Attraction

The perpetual transmutation element of this law holds that everything is in a constant state of change – energy is always moving in and out of form of some kind. We alone choose how we will direct our power.

The Law of Gratitude

Gratitude is a high-energy positive vibration of thought. It keeps us connected to power.

The grateful mind is constantly fixed on the best. When we're grateful about everything, we focus on receiving more of those things into our lives. It's not easy to see the good around us in the midst of struggle, and yet the ability to do so generates a high-energy vibration that helps make great things happen. Identify all that you are grateful for in your self and your life.

An attitude of gratitude ensures that our highest possible positive energy is focused on receiving. As Wallace Wattles puts it, "People who can sincerely be thankful for things which they own only in imagination have real *faith*. They will get rich; they will cause the creation of whatever they want."

The Law of Relativity/Non-resistance

Everything is relative.

Think of this in terms of vibration. What do we know about vibration? That rates of vibration are either high or low *only in comparison with other rates of vibration*. They are relative to one another.

When this law is properly followed, you win because it's all about perception. For example, everyone does something better than you. Likewise, you do something better than everyone else. If you compare yourself with someone who does something better than you, for whatever reason, you can't help but feel bad. Remind yourself it is what it is relative to everything else. It's how you judge reality that influences your own self-perceptions. Instead of focusing on what others have that you don't, increase your self-awareness; understand your values so you can focus on being your best, too. When you allow other people's reality to let you feel bad about your own, you're using the law of relativity against yourself. Use it instead to heighten your self-esteem. You'll become aware of how special you are in the light of truth. Shelf the clutter long enough so you can focus on the challenge or opportunity at hand.

This law is also called the law of non-resistance: Stop fighting or worrying about things and stay forward-focused. Let's be honest. Most people go through life thinking things should be different. This usually applies, in their mind, to people's behavior and circumstances, which are beyond their ability to change. The law of non-resistance reminds us it's useless to waste our time arguing with reality for being the way it is. I know I justify my arguments with reality by believing they're about principle. This just ends up hurting me, though, because I can't change other people. When I try to change them, I'm wasting energy that I could direct toward bringing me the results I do want. I keep trying to manage my distractions better and deal with my feelings through continual focus.

Rather than descending into unproductive approaches, we can choose to apply one of the other universal laws to the situation. For example, the law of opposites, or polarity. The law of opposites simply states that everything has two equal and opposite sides. Every situation that looks bad has an equal amount of good; we just have to find it.

There are two ways to apply the law of non-resistance and move on. The first is to keep in mind that *the universe is friendly to our objectives*. Focus on remembering that there's an infinite supply of everything we need. There's enough for you, whether money, customers, time, opportunity, romantic partners, or friends. The universe is friendly and wants us to be happy. No situation can leave you without these things for long.

The second is to remember that *you get to decide how you want to view the situation, good or bad, because it just is*. Focusing on rolling with it and not fighting speeds up the process and gets you to the good part faster. Focus on finding the good in situations, and be thankful for it. By doing this, you shift the energy to what you want. This isn't an excuse to do nothing. It calls you to be where you are and focus on your new reality, which is waiting for you just down the path if you seek it.

Everything that happens, happens for a reason. If you take the time to really understand this, you'll have the power to make dramatic changes in your paradigms, perceptions, and reality.

The Law of Vibration

Everything in the universe vibrates ... nothing rests. We really do live in an ocean of motion.

We may understand this idea of vibrations by considering our feelings. Good feelings have a higher vibration than negative ones. The more conscious we are of our feelings, the better we can direct them for our gain and get to the better parts of our journey. Our thoughts are another form of vibration we send off into the universe. When we focus, our vibrations are stronger. When we're thoughtful of others around us, our vibrations are also stronger. Do you see how it goes? Our thoughts are cosmic waves of energy. *Thought* is the most potent vibration, so think about your objectives for your life and perfect your visions in your thoughts, and then make it happen.

The Law of Polarity

Everything in the universe has its opposite. There's no inside to a room without an outside. You have a right and left side to your body, a front and back. Every up has a down and every down has an up.

The law of polarity takes this reality further. It states that everything not only has an opposite, but this opposite is *equal*. If it's three feet from the floor to the table, it's three feet from the table to the floor. If it's 150 miles from Brussels to Liège, it's 150 miles from Liège to Brussels.

If something happens in your life that you consider bad, there has to be something good about it. If it was only a little bad, you'll see it was only a little good.

The Law of Rhythm

The law of rhythm embodies the truth that everything is moving to and fro, flowing in and out, swinging backward and forward. There's a reaction to every action. Something must advance when something retreats; something must rise when something sinks.

The law of rhythm is universal as observed in the rising and setting of the sun, the ebb and flow of the tides, the coming and going of the seasons, and our levels of consciousness.

You're not going to feel good all of the time; no one does. If you did, you wouldn't even know it: Low feelings are what permit you to enjoy high feelings.

There will always be highs and lows in life. We choose how we respond to what is. Even in the midst of a downswing, we can choose good thoughts and continue to move up toward our goal. Focus on the rhythm with which you want to move your life and always work to get back to that. It will happen, because you control your rate of vibration, energy, and thoughts.

The Law of Cause and Effect

Every cause has an effect; every effect has a cause. There's no such thing as chance. Everything happens according to law. Nothing in the entire universe ever happens outside the laws of the universe. The universe and its laws bring predictability to life.

We live in a perpetual, never-ending cycle of cause and effect. Ralph Waldo Emerson called the law of cause and effect "the law of laws."

We're all very interested in results: our physical health, our relationships, the respect we earn for who we are, and our material income. Concentrate on what you want – the cause – and the effect will soon follow. As the law makes clear, for every action there is always a consequence that can't be escaped. So when you choose better actions, you'll experience better consequences and realize your desired effect sooner. *Karma* is the ancient Eastern belief that what you do will come back to you. If your actions are good on a day-to-day basis, you'll have good karma (effects). If your actions are bad, you'll experience bad karma (effects). Your actions create your effects.

In a cause-and-effect universe, every thought and action we plant comes back to us multiplied.

The Law of Manifestation

According to this law, we create our reality with our words, thoughts, and actions.

Here's how the sequence goes. First comes the word that prompts the thought, then the idea that produces action. All three – words, thoughts, action – produce a result, which we experience. The most important of the three is intentional action: action, that is, that comes from purposeful words and thoughts. Emotion is energy in motion that propels us to take action.

The Law of Infinite Possibilities

Being connected, as all of us are, to a source, we exist in a field of pure potentiality. Anything is possible. The only limits to what we can achieve come from our own recordings and the restrictions we put on ourselves through our limiting beliefs. We can be and do anything, unless we think otherwise.

The Thinking Part

When you change your beliefs, your life will change. The laws we have explored focus on our thinking because everything in this world we see begins with thought. The only way we can make real changes is to start with the thinking part. Feelings are not thoughts; they are feelings. They inform you, but not the universe. Don't get stuck in your emotions; instead, use them to inform thoughts and then direct them to have better effects.

Even thinking is not enough, however. To effect real change, your actions must change.

The most successful people focus on the process being used to realize results, not on the specific result they're after. The result achieved is a natural outcome of doing the process well. By extension, therefore, the more we incorporate the process of self-awareness, focus, and strategy, the more consistently we will realize success. If our minds are anywhere and everywhere but in the moment, this lack of focus will limit gains that are otherwise possible for us.

These laws give all of us the same opportunity to realize success. These laws are all about how we focus our thoughts, energies, and intentions; this is the internal focus that enables us to achieve whatever we desire. Of course it's possible to achieve success without consciously following the laws, but why would we do that when these laws can only complement our self-awareness to make living easier and our strategies more effective?

WHAT ABOUT YOU?

- *If you believed that one of these laws could most benefit you, right now, where you are, which one would it be?*

- *What are you trying to force?*

- *What if you didn't and trusted more? Could you?*

- *Pick just one area where your efforts to control are draining you of your energy. How are you currently channeling your thoughts? (law of vibration)*

- *Where would more perspective allow you to push on? (law of polarity)*

- *What do you allow to suck you in and take your eyes off your focus? (law of rhythm)*

- *What are the effects that you have caused, and not yet addressed?*

- *What do you notice that you think about the most? (law of manifestation)*

- *What are some of your unfulfilled possibilities?*

Part 4

Success

$$\begin{array}{r} \textit{Self-Awareness} \\ \boldsymbol{+} \qquad \textit{Focus} \\ \boldsymbol{+} \qquad \textit{Strategy} \\ \hline \boldsymbol{= SUCCESS} \end{array}$$

Chapter 14

Objectives

*Success follows doing
what you want to do.
There is no other way
to be successful.*

–Malcolm Forbes

T'S time to tie together all of the
pieces that lead to the destination we call
success. *Success* is the result of putting
self-awareness into action and making
better choices. *Focus* will help you direct
your attention, and *strategy* will deliver
success.

Life is always about reaching objectives and therefore is always about
success. The clearer we are on the
purpose behind our actions, the more
concrete our progress will be. Don't be
afraid to set standards. Instead, commit

to honoring them. Focus on what having them will net you. This is part of living your birthright of joy, peace, fulfillment, and success.

Owning Our Success

Everything around us has been designed or developed to support us in realizing our objectives. For example, if we need access to people and markets and have no idea how to reach them, the Internet is available to help us find a path. It's already there, waiting for us to tap for our maximum gain. If we need to get somewhere and have car problems, there are buses we can take, or people we can ask to drive us. There are always options. We just have to use our awareness of what we want as we creatively choose.

While we're set up to succeed, we have an ownership piece in making it happen. Success is not the result of wishing on the same star daily. Success is always a function of strategic focus and self-awareness. The beautiful part – the part we don't seem to easily get – is that we're responsible only for who we are, the choices we make, and the way we treat others.

Knowing Your Destiny

Your destiny may not be to lead the firm.

Danny didn't realize this about himself, at first. He decided being a business leader was his destiny and made his choices accordingly. He fast-tracked to the role of Chief Operations Officer and was ready to assume the CEO position, which was soon to become vacant. It wasn't happening fast enough for Danny, though. When he and I met at a business function, he said he wanted to explore the profiling of his natural self.

In our work together, I held the mirror up to him and

asked him challenging questions about the results he was accepting and the role his slow, deliberate focus was playing in the overall effectiveness of his organization. Danny, at times in tears, hated the image he was seeing. It was great to witness Danny's courage to be with his own truth so he could consider whether he wanted to make changes.

It's not as if Danny wasn't aware of some of his key challenges; he knew they were stressing him out. He was trying to operate as someone he wasn't and at a pace that wasn't natural for him. He didn't *need* to be the CEO. He had just got caught-up in what everyone had always told him about himself. They were right. He *is* brilliant as the number two guy. That's why they made him COO. And Danny had to admit it was the role he was most passionate about playing.

High performance is excellence, and the greater the alignment between our being and doing, the greater the likelihood we'll achieve excellence.

Don't make yourself write with your left hand all day if you're naturally right-handed. Focus on figuring out what you can do effortlessly with your right hand. You'll baulk at these simple words if you're living from the outside in. It just boils down to how you want your approach to leave you feeling. The results will always get better when you focus more on being who you are. You always get to choose: You can either actively engage with the journey of your life, as a work in progress, or tolerate an unfulfilling life.

There's no straight path to realizing much in life, and that's okay: The detours make life exciting and develop character.

The clearer you can be on your values, strengths, and blind spots, the better equipped you'll be to deal with the obstacles in your path caused by other people's actions. Success is directly related to the degree to which you have realized your objectives. You're living successfully when your objectives reflect what you value and desire. You're the only one who can know and define your objectives. Trying to run with someone else's vision will only net you mediocre to good results, unless you can find your values in those visions.

In Pursuit of Results

I had a discussion with someone in the coffee shop today about results and risk. He had come to Canada from the Orient, leaving everything familiar behind – his extended family, job, language, and culture – so he and his family could experience a better life.

"You're obviously a risk-taker," I said.

"No way," he said. "I've been in Canada for the past thirty years and have just lived my life."

When I held the mirror up for him over a quick coffee, he acknowledged the huge results he has achieved in his life and the risks he took to achieve them, including leaving all that was familiar and comfortable.

He paused for a few minutes. This was definitely not the way he pictured himself. He smiled and said he liked the idea but still believed he wasn't a risk-taker. Necessity had driven him, he said.

I'm not so sure. Not everyone in similar circumstances has the courage to willingly move forward the way he did.

Regardless of how conscious we are of the fact, we're always in pursuit of results and that pursuit always includes risk. Everything we do is with an objective in mind. If you considered all of the risks you have taken successfully in your life, small or big, daily or annually, would you take on more risks or cut back? In every minute of every day we're making choices. Choosing is risky. Just acknowledge you make choices and bask in the feeling you get for making them well.

You have more in you to realize. Stop being like the china you take out only for special occasions; celebrate that you have it and use it. We've got what we've got to be used.

Rumor is, if we don't use it we'll lose it. The more actively we engage with our lives, the more successful we will be.

Defining Standards

The world tells us having money equals success. It's no wonder so many of us focus on material gains.

It's lazy to use the world's standards and dismiss your own definition of success, though. Define your own standards and have the courage to live in integrity to them. They're perfect and right because they come from within you. Something bigger, better, and smarter than you designed you. Trust it. You don't try to override the brake system on your vehicle. Why try to override the engineer who guides the evolutionary path that fits your design?

We're all meant to enjoy this beautiful world, and money enables us to do so. Financial gain is one part of the journey we can all expect to make advances on throughout our lives. So just know that. And, even if only for a moment, put that focus to the side. Now think about enjoying the world on your terms, doing what you're great at with a person or people you enjoy. What do you need to be doing differently to make that happen? What do you still need to learn about yourself to perform better at the things you're doing? What more do you need to learn about yourself or something else to focus in a new way?

WHAT ABOUT YOU?

- *How satisfied are you with your current levels of success?*

- *What do you need more of to feel successful?*

- *What will that then give you?*

- *What feeling are you pursuing "fullness" for?*

Chapter 15

Success Stories

What would life be if we had no courage to attempt anything?

–Vincent van Gogh

Success can require hours and hours of long hard work – or not. In any event, it requires believing in what you're doing. The more conviction you have in reaching your objective, the easier it will be for you to deal with the setbacks that come up (and they always will).

Are you really living for what you believe in?

Let's look in on Bill, Louis, and Rick, real-life examples of clients who are actively increasing their own personal awareness for a more meaningful and successful journey.

A New Bill

Bill heads up a big manufacturing firm. He's quite successful. He has a big house, cottages, beautiful kids, and a trophy wife and is respected in the business community.

One night I was at the grocery store as it was closing. As my purchases were being bagged, I heard a commotion two checkout aisles down. To my surprise, there was Bill yelling at a cashier because she was insisting on a store policy.

As he threw his armful of purchases to the floor, Bill caught sight of me. As you can imagine, he was quite embarrassed. He seemed to be jolted into realizing that others were still in the store. He apologized to the cashier and left, not acknowledging me when he passed. He apologized to me, too, in our next session.

In our work together, there was one specific portfolio that caused Bill angst. He couldn't put his finger on what was amiss. His general sense was that he was losing his edge and being less of a leader. He was confused by this. He knew the board was not displeased – no one was saying much – but that didn't matter, because *he* knew.

Optics were important to Bill. He tended to live life from the outside in, based on external expectations, rather than from the inside out, based on his own wants and needs. He had always taken the former approach because the benefits were easier to see. He got more ego strokes because he was so good at doing what people expected him to do. He was paying the price for following this approach, however. It's no wonder he felt he was getting stale.

We did make progress. Bill began to tease out what was making him less effective and less confident. He had bought into the social welfare system in which the man is the provider who denies self for family. He never questioned the impact on his being of ignoring personal questions about his purpose and identity. His values were just things in his daydreams. He never thought of allowing them to inform his personal leadership, and as a result, Bill had lost the bounce in his step.

When Bill considered personal leadership, it put him a little off kilter. He had spent most of his adult years trying to establish an identity for himself as a provider and a brilliant businessman, never acknowledging much about who he was. As he began putting meaning into some of the adjectives he liked most, he saw the opportunity to incorporate those values into his overall leadership as a way of growing.

Bill and I went through a very helpful exercise together. Using case studies and real-life situations, he considered objectively what he brought to the table when he was being a *good* CEO. This included achieving the majority of his key objectives and holding people accountable sporadically. It meant tolerating a few on his leadership team who weren't so strong. Aiming for the good allowed him to come in later on some days than others and maybe even have a couple of glasses of wine at lunch.

We went through the same exercise to see what he needed to bring into his work to be a *great* CEO. Bill didn't react emotionally as he considered this question. He saw how he could step up in his communication style. Currently he was communicating very little. His loosely connected expectations removed the need to hold people accountable. Mediocrity seemed good enough for everyone.

As a result of our work together, Bill tapped back into his results orientation to complement his big-picture style. He engaged strategically, which included an active search for better talent, using agencies such as The Staffing Edge. He delegated and communicated more strategically and began to empower his troops in the field again.

Bill also started to bring more specific values, such as integrity, to his leadership style. He took this value beyond being just a word to being a mindset because he knew he wasn't being vigilant about his leadership and life. He focused on who he was in light of his values and raised his own bar on what it meant to be Bill. He allowed himself to assert for more standards in all of his life, always factoring in more self-awareness. Today, his strategies are better informed for it. He's feeling more successful and his company is realizing better results.

Awareness focusing isn't complicated. It does require effort as we acknowledge things as they really are vs. how we're told to see things. It takes courage, open mindedness, and faith.

The old Bill had not been through any action-reflection learning. He had become a one-person show. The new Bill cast a wider net to capture better results.

Randy the Short-Termer

Randy wasn't broken. He had accepted his lot in life and his role in having created it. Now he wanted to develop strategies for realizing more fulfillment and self-satisfaction. He was known for his high IQ, his wit, his prowess as a conversationalist, and his insight. Even if he wasn't these things, he still deserved to be happy. We all do.

The walls were closing in on Randy. He was north of fifty and was becoming increasingly aware of the ineffectiveness of his life strategy: His job, company, colleagues, clients, and family were his reminders.

Randy came to me to develop a new vision. He was desperate to work on this because he definitely wanted more for his life.

The world needs Randy types: He was a good guy with a mild personality. He was effective enough in his work. Not everyone has to be hard-driving and intense. Unfortunately, Randy had felt dissatisfied with his life and his job most of his life, and had been taking on lovers to help him get through some of his displeasure. It was a short-term strategy to help him deal with the reality that had become his life. Physical intimacy is something he values and he has a sincere love of women, short/tall, big/slim. He cares about people. Randy made his choices for the short term: what felt good right now and what offered big payouts.

Randy's wife had learned of his infidelities, and he had been spending the last ten years trying to earn back her respect and trust. Divorce wasn't an option for either of them. Having lived for the short term, their cash flow was meager and their savings even worse. So they stayed in their unfulfilling marriage. She needed his money and he needed her to stay so he wouldn't have to pay alimony payments. What a sad existence! Randy had always wanted more and had never figured out how to get there. He felt no conviction for anything, except intellect. He had learned to work around his empty marriage. He wanted better results and more success in his life. Even so, he couldn't find the conviction to stick with anything.

Randy's master strategy was to take the easiest, safest path: bringing value to others. This strategy is similar to that of many philanthropists. It's easy for them to think their works will fill the void caused by their lack of being. Randy couldn't really do much about his weak foundations and so built on top of them.

It was so impressive to see Randy summon the courage to articulate his questions and pursue a solid understanding of who he is. He was taking the first step in realizing success.

Randy is a good example of how acknowledging the questions we're struggling with isn't enough. While we may eventually demand answers for these questions, it's not a given that we will and therefore that our lives will be better for them. This is the piece Randy wrestled with the most. At first he asked questions about possibilities only to himself, in his head. The learning, the growth, the progress, the success, the fulfillment, the joy, the possibilities – you name it – all of these became possible for him only as he considered the choices in front of him and then began to make them and act on them. He started with where the best ROI was possible: turning up the business-development dial. This was a good place to begin because it addressed a huge pressure he was feeling.

Unless we ask, unless we acknowledge, unless we care, how can we move closer to our desired reality? How do we get unstuck?

The Real Louis

Louis is a high-powered litigation lawyer, a senior partner with an impressive reputation. Ironically, though he commanded much respect in the courtroom, he wasn't commanding any personal respect for himself.

The situation Louis found himself in highlighted to me how key self-awareness is to fulfillment and success.

I soon realized Louis was passive aggressive. As a strategy, he told himself to hold his cards close to his chest and just observe. Then some arbitrary action would make him explode. Nevertheless, I was beginning to get a glimpse of some values that were important to him concerning justice and excellence.

It's natural for high-achieving individuals such as Louis to be more aware of their effectiveness than of themselves. It's fascinating to see so many intelligent, capable people live lives focused on others' perceptions of them, or define themselves by the value they bring to others. We bring most value to the world when we focus on our design. We receive most benefits from being who we are.

Other lawyers hated being up against Louis in court. He was solid, strong, and always won. However, even though he was bringing value to his clients, he was easily agitated and rarely satisfied. Being praised provoked him.

In our work together, we focused on increasing his

self-satisfaction, self-awareness, and fulfillment. As he got clearer on the values that inspired and drove him, he engaged a few of them: compassion, perspective, and health. He understood that praise provoked him because excellence was not a value he identified with. He did what he did out of his strong views about justice. Most of the values he had been holding on to were instilled in him earlier in life and had never been challenged or examined. As Socrates said so long ago, "The unexamined life is not worth living." I think that's another way of pointing to the joy the examined life offers. Seeing the difference self-examination makes, why would you not take this approach?

Following our sessions, Louis was as well prepared as ever and continued winning his cases. However, as he gave more thought to his person and began considering who he was *outside* the courtroom, he respected himself more – and was respected more by others.

This is a gradual process for Louis because he needs to examine each value through the filter of his leading value: **integrity**. Now he lets himself appreciate the value he's bringing to his law firm. He's happier because he's giving himself permission to be happier. For Louis, the permission piece was powerful. He is naturally more detail oriented. Now he knows that allowing himself to consider things from the big-picture perspective, as his intuition guides him, is helping him gain more personal control in his life.

WHAT ABOUT YOU?

- *What questions are you avoiding?*

- *For what reason do you avoid going there?*

- *What are the worst-case-scenario consequences of knowing?*

- *What are the consequences, in the life you're living now, of not acknowledging your questions?*

- *How do you feel about your approach?*

- *How likely is it that you will continue on this same road?*

- *What are you afraid of?*

- *Which of your values help you minimize this fear?*

- *Are you more focused on the possibilities or the worst-case scenarios?*

Chapter 16

Success Is Not for Sissies

In reading the lives of great men, I found that the first victory they won was over themselves ... self-discipline with all of them came first.

–Harry S. Truman

WHEN I work with clients, we focus on corporate objectives. We also look at personal satisfaction levels and where there might be room for growth. All the while I'm working hard to understand the people in front of me. I want to know what drives them and how to challenge and push them. This process gives them a clearer understanding of who they are and enables them to consider themselves in deeper, more strategic ways. They welcome a perspective that considers and factors in their personal pressures and responsibilities because *who they are* seems to have lost relevance. Their existence has become defined by their doing, rather than their being. That strategy could be effective, if we were human *doings*. Focusing on our *being* will bring us greater success and fulfillment in our *doing*.

A Story of Courage: Seth

Real change is not for sissies, and Seth is no sissy. He's a likable fellow, the kind of guy you might want your son to be like.

Seth knew he wanted a better life. He had made his share of personal decisions that were continuing to affect his life. His decisions tended to favor the short term with only a big-picture glance at how the long term might look. He wanted people to think his life was enviable. Giving it the old college try, he faked much of his life, living without integrity to himself or anyone else.

As is often true of people in his kind of situation, his health was a concern. He had a drinking problem and was getting bigger and bigger. Those around him didn't really care because he was meeting their tangible needs. He was financially comfortable and already had everything his world could give him.

Seth and his buddies formed an unofficial boys club, showing up for family things only when it was visible to others and helped them maintain their façade.

Seth didn't want this for himself anymore. He wanted to make changes. He was so hardwired by the outside world, he wasn't really sure an inside vision was even possible.

There was much creative tension in his life. He knew he wanted a fulfilling life and saw no way out of his existing reality. He was conflicted between the shoulds – the dogmatic requirements of our society of a man with young kids and a stay-at-home wife – and his own feelings.

Without knowing how else to make changes that would be acceptable to others, Seth decided to act and ended up changing his whole life. He was able to summon up faith and develop a vision to be more engaged with his life, at a deeper level. He quit the job that did not stimulate his intellect. He established standards with his children for more respect. He demanded that his wife take more responsibility for her own life. He stopped drinking and stopped participating in the lie he was afraid to confront.

Not everyone in Seth's sphere of influence valued his choices. His buddies and even his spouse missed the drinking parties. His kids had no desire to give him more respect. Eventually his wife had an affair and divorced Seth, draining him of his retirement savings.

In the midst of it all, Seth stayed with his commitment to courage. He focused relentlessly on what he believed was possible for him. He got clearer on what he valued most, which made him realize most of his life was not enough for him if he was to be the person he really is.

Before he got to this point, though, Seth had to challenge all of his beliefs – everything he thought was real – and to determine what he wanted his life to be about.

Not only did Seth challenge the systems all around him, he stopped letting others dictate how he was to live. He took huge hits for this. He lost much. He continues to stand by his decisions because he has never felt so good. His faith serves him well here, because the challenges aren't letting up. Seth is getting exactly what he started the process for: fulfillment, peace, and satisfaction. He is strong and will rise again. In the interim, he still outperforms most people because of his strong work ethic.

The integrity that had been lacking in his life reared its head throughout the process. He always had to answer the questions, "Is it worth it?" "What am I doing?" "Was I wrong?"

Seth is not the norm. His changes were so huge, his struggle so challenging, and yet he had the courage to stay the course. Had he not taken the risks and made the changes, however sloppily he may have done so, he would still be where he was – unhappy and dissatisfied at his deepest levels, with little likelihood of finding his *"more."*

A Story of Determination: Maggie

Maggie was quite a different case – or maybe not. She didn't know exactly what she wanted, only that she would implode if she didn't do *something* about her life. She had contacted several different executive coaches. She had left a message for me, mentioning the name of her organization and the name of the colleague who had recommended she see me.

I had never worked with her colleague and was surprised by the referral. Maggie and I exchanged a few e-mails and spoke on the telephone. I was beginning to get a sense of who she was.

I told her my firm doesn't engage with clients without seeing their profile first. I've been using the same profiling system with clients for over four years now and it is powerful. As a trained expert in this psychometric tool, I'm able to quickly get a sense of the values that drive a person. This tool helps me know how likely they are to respond to the process I take my clients through to achieve results. This is important information for me, because I've worked with too many clients and companies that expect me to change their blue-eyed employees into brown-eyed ones.

In this case, no hocus-pocus was being asked of me. Maggie had been brought into my life for a reason. We began our work together.

Maggie, forty-seven years old, is a beautiful, intelligent,

strong woman. She has a significant leadership role. However, while challenging and stimulating intellectually, this role was not enough for her. She wanted more. Being Indo-Canadian helps me relate to other ambitious women who have to deal with being non-white women in a white man's world.

Maggie was all business. I could see she was trying to read me. That isn't unusual at the beginning of my engagements. The clients who end up in front of me are there because they want growth and more success. They're ready to challenge their mindset and the processes around them. They've proven to themselves they can play the game and be effective. Now they're ready to put that game on hold to find a new strategy and process for approaching the same opportunity or maybe even for shaking things up and regrouping. As a result, when they meet me they're not always sure what they're getting themselves into. They're not sure I can make a difference. They may feel I don't look old enough or "corporate" enough. (I don't own very many black or blue pinstripe suits.)

Maggie jumped right into our engagement. She shared how she and her husband just coexisted. How her life revolved around her work. How she had allowed herself to become isolated and friendless. Kids were not on her radar. She didn't come to coaching with any regrets for the choices she had made but because she was ready for more of life and more of herself. She didn't attribute this desire to anything specific; she just felt an internal gnawing and knew she no longer wanted to continue living the way she had.

I was so impressed by her knowingness, her courage, and her commitment to personal excellence for self. She could have rested on her laurels. Her shareholders were content. She could have been content, too, taking it easy and just enjoying her current success. But her body was sending her non-stop signals of dis-ease – one of the many nudges that were making her willing and ready.

Maggie challenged every conceivable process you could imagine. She was ready to see her life clearly and honestly. She defined her must-have values and measured her life against them. She was shocked to see that not one of the values that most mattered to her was being supported by her choices.

Change was the only option. As she was gaining clarity about her needs and desires, she embraced her need for intensity and energy. Our focus shifted to a strategy of managing the change she was creating in her life.

As most of my clients do, Maggie came with a focus on being a better leader. She saw this required her to first be a better Maggie. After clarifying for herself what she most valued, she committed herself to what was most important to her. She embraced this challenge and kept her focus on painting the bigger-picture possibilities of her life even though she was naturally more detail-focused.

I was very impressed by Maggie's courage to journey inside herself more deeply with each successive week. She was exhausted by the changes she was bringing into her life. Because integrity was important to her, she couldn't let more of her life go by with only marginal changes. As she acted in integrity, she began to take on a spirit of energy and lightness.

Maggie took on a more satisfying role as a short-term strategy and started considering new careers for herself. She got her own place and made changes to her dress, hair, and style, to better capture her spirit.

A Story of Growth: Tim

Tim is a serial restaurateur. Perhaps they're all that way; it's certainly a type of business one must be hardwired for. Or is it? Tim has played the role very effectively with a string of successful restaurants for over thirty years.

When we met, he offered that he didn't enjoy the process of going from business opportunity to business opportunity, even though he did so with vigor. When he came to work with me, he had decided to focus on one restaurant and be willing to accept how that played out for him. His nomadic years were over – he just wasn't sure how he would spend the years left to him.

I loved working with Tim because of how clear he was about his life and how willing he was to grow. He said he had reached this chapter of his life feeling more relaxed than he had in thirty years. I asked him what the tradeoffs were for him in taking this new approach. He explained in depth how much he was *gaining* from his new approach. Tim's story is full of helpful insights:

1 Tim had spent most of his life in situations and pursuits that, however draining, were so profitable there was no real opportunity, energy, or rationale to justify focusing differently. Good was the enemy of great. Like so many of us, he was caught in the tension between the demands of life and his own needs.

2 The tendency of an achiever is to consider self only after a certain age, or after certain milestones have been accomplished. This is a sound approach *if* living with fulfillment doesn't have to be suspended until then. With a little creativity, you can satisfy more of your must-haves, starting now.

3 We really do know what's best for us, it's just that it takes increased self-awareness for us to see more clearly what we're doing and what the tradeoffs of our choices are and whether the tradeoffs are worth it. Tim had experienced a successful career according to the external measurements he cross-referenced.

To me – and Tim embraced this philosophy – people who have achieved so much are ripe for much greater personal success. If they can do so well when they factor very little information regarding self into their decisions, the sky's the limit for them when that becomes the main way they approach life.

Sometimes people think bringing their own needs into the equation will just cause them problems. Is that what your actions reveal? Without trying the road to self-awareness, strategically, how can you know? As I've found in my life and seen in the lives of my clients, the more we know about ourselves and apply that knowledge to our pursuits, the more likely we are to have the Midas touch in the whole of our lives.

WHAT ABOUT YOU?

- *What's the success you want most in your life?*
  At your body level, your mind level, and your soul level?

- *What strategies have you put in place to achieve success in these areas?*

- *What do you have conviction for?*

- *Are you successful in the area of your life associated with this conviction?*

- *How successful are you at being in integrity to yourself?*

Chapter 17

What Coaching Can Do for You

The most important, and indeed the truly unique, contribution of management in the twentieth century was the fifty-fold increase in the productivity of the manual worker in manufacturing. The most important contribution management needs to make in the twenty-first century is similarly to increase the productivity of knowledge work and the knowledge worker.

–Peter Drucker

THROUGHOUT this book I've shared stories with you, as well as my formula. Personal awareness *is* the conduit to realizing more excellence in life and work. My hope in this chapter is to show you that, although you can make progress on your own, the best way to achieve sustainable change is with a neutral third party like a coach.

Working with a Coach

I'm increasingly persuaded of how valuable it is for people to work with a coach if they want a different path to achieve better and different results in their life and work. The process is valuable for many reasons but primarily, I think, because of the objectivity a trained professional can offer. An unbiased, objective third party can help clients to finally focus on their own life in the midst of all the busyness they're experiencing.

It's best to begin working with a coach when you have a sense of the results you're looking for. There are coaches who primarily support people in their personal growth. Many people – and I'm one of them – want a coach to work with them on their professional and personal growth and help them advance toward specific objectives. Know what you want more of in your life and find a coach who has proven effectiveness in helping people achieve those results. Credentials are of secondary importance. Look for the risks they've taken in their own life, in all areas of their life, and the results they've achieved. Look at the values in their life that could help you grow and learn. Make sure your hairdresser doesn't have the worst hair.

In the botanical world, the higher up the tree, the better the fruit. It's easier to reach the *good* fruit at the bottom of the tree, the kind everyone has because they don't have a process to keep climbing. To get the *great* fruit, you're going to have to climb. The same is true in your life. If you want to enjoy the best, to reach the top of what's possible in your life, you're going to have to work harder. It will take longer for you to reach the top. As this book has shown, it takes intense focus on what really matters to you – and a strategy.

Here's the interesting part: En route to the best fruit, you'll become more familiar with the tree and the process you're taking to get to the top. This will increase your knowledge and help you climb more efficiently and effectively.

What does coaching have to do with this? Simply that you need someone to hold the ladder for you as you climb. We can't reach the best within ourselves on our own. Coaching creates opportunities we otherwise would censor or perhaps not even see.

The coaching conversation remains the most important tool I use to support my clients. It's an objective way to challenge a client to reach higher objectives and grow as they raise their awareness. Working with a coach will assist you as you shine light on the consequences of your behaviors and gauge where you may still want to go and how you're going to get there.

Coaching will increase your comfort and expertise in exploring different perspectives. "What if" thinking will help you consider the difference it would make to your life if more of *you* was present. The more willing you are to reevaluate, revise, and refocus specific efforts for conscious results, the more likely you'll reach meaningful objectives with excellence.

Finding a coach is easy; finding the *right* coach – the right one for you, the one you really need; one who can and will push you forward to help you achieve your specific results – can be a challenge.

Coaches are growing in number, and the majority of us are trained and certified. We want to see more and more people living lives they enjoy and with more personal control.

If that is what you're primarily interested in, find a coach with whom you connect. The Internet abounds with coaches, or you can ask for contacts from those in your sphere. You may be surprised by how many of the people you know are working with a coach or have done so recently. This kind of professional and personal development is a private journey. Information about it may not be volunteered unless you ask.

As mentioned earlier in this book, there are those who call themselves coaches and act primarily as the expert. That is consulting. In a true coaching initiative the client is the expert and the coach enables the client to realize new and different results.

Start looking. Select a coach based on your objective for the initiative and the pace of learning you prefer. Remember, the focus is not that you *need* a coach because you're deficient but that you *want* one to help you get to the next level of excellence.

People who are already good know they need help to reach new gains and heights. Here are two questions to ask yourself in deciding whether you want to work with a coach:

Question #1:
Am I achieving the results I know I'm capable of in my life?

Question #2:
Do I care?

If you don't care about what you're doing, address that first. Go find something you *do* care about, or work with a coach. Life is too short! Begin to identify what would jazz you up and cover your expenses.

If you're not satisfied with the results you're producing, ask yourself what processes you're going to introduce to change your personal levels of satisfaction.

I haven't claimed in this book or with any of my clients to be an expert in running their business. My expertise comes from living my secret – **Self-Awareness + Focus + Strategy = Success** – and sharing this with others.

Informing Your Strategies

I ask again: What about you? Unless your strategies are informed and influenced by your knowledge and ability to understand the inside of your organization, how comfortable can you, as a CEO, be in spending all that time and $$ in execution?

How informed are your strategies – both personal and professional? How is that working for you?

It's lonely at the top. It's tough for you to get to the next level without honest, unbiased feedback and challenges to your logic. Avoid trying to be your own best advisor. Sustainable success requires self-awareness. Find someone to help you develop that awareness. Engage the right coach to help you discover more of your potential, even if only to help you get familiar with how the process of personal growth and increased self-awareness works and where and how you can use it.

If you want to be more of a leader, seek credible, critical, and challenging third-party objectivity. The world needs you – needs all of us – to evolve and be held accountable to reach higher standards.

About Sheeba Varghese and Forward Focus Inc.

I started Forward Focus Inc. in 2002 with a three-fold focus: helping key leaders to refocus their already sharpened skills for maximum alignment with their values; working with people to clarify their values and factor them into their personal performance and satisfaction; and increasing the results of my clients' organizations.

I function as a bilingual executive coach in English and French and work with CEOs and senior executives in new industries/markets, such as financial services, stock exchanges, oil and gas, mining, investment banking, and professional sport. I also have clients from the retail sector, arts, environmental services, education, government, health care, hospitality, legal, media, packaging, and executive search.

Forward Focus Inc. works with leadership teams of Fortune 500 companies, salespeople, directors, senior execs, and CEOs. The firm's clients come primarily from the private sector, though we have worked with teams of public sector senior executives and directors. My clients have included engineers, chemists, lawyers, academics, psychologists, Chartered Accountants, entrepreneurs, national managers, doctors, and MBA graduates.

I've served these clients in cities across North America, including Baltimore, California, Calgary, Cleveland, Halifax, Montreal, New York, Toronto, and Washington D.C. Forward Focus Inc. has contracts pending in India, South America, and Switzerland. These opportunities are a direct result of the international alliances the company has formed with organizations such as Korn/Ferry International.

Generally speaking, my clients tend to come to the coaching initiative wanting to enhance their performance, expecting that coaching will improve their overall satisfaction and effectiveness. They're open to exploring the connection between their level of personal fulfillment and their performance. To date, I've targeted only high performers and leading institutions. With the aid of leading edge technology, I offer very specific, relevant insights and data to my clients for maximum success in their business and life.

The objectives for each client initiative are determined by the client after we review their overall objectives for self. The objectives are always focused on high performance and excellence.

Forward Focus Inc.
241 Littlewood
Oakville, Ontario, Canada
L6H 7Z1

E-mail: info@forwardfocus.ca
Phone: 1-866-737-7188

Sheeba can be reached directly via her blog www.Sheeba.com or @sheebascorner (Twitter)

CPSIA information can be obtained at www.ICGtesting.com
Printed in the USA
245447LV00010B/1/P